THE FLOWERS OF EVIL

CHARLES BAUDELAIRE

TRANSLATED BY RICHARD HOWARD

GODINE

BOSTON

Published in 2025 by
GODINE
Boston, Massachusetts

LIBRARY OF CONGRESS CONTROL NUMBER 2021950663
ISBN 978-1-56792-827-3

Second Printing, 2025
Printed in the United States of America

"... a translation comes later than the original, and since the important works of world literature never find their chosen translators at the time of their origin, their translation marks their stage of continued life."

—Walter Benjamin

from "The Task of the Translator," introduction to his translation of Baudelaire, 1923

CONTENTS

THE FLOWERS OF EVIL

SPLEEN AND IDEAL

PARISIAN SCENES

WINE

FLOWERS OF EVIL

REBELLION

DEATH

ADDITIONAL POEMS

FOREWORD

H ERE IS ONE MORE translation of Baudelaire's poetry. If
the reader is tempted to smile, I can avow I smile as well
(and if to sigh, even so…); it is for such a reader I would express
here the principles to which that smile appeals.

It is a translation of the whole of *Les Fleurs du Mal* with twenty
additional poems not included in either edition published in the
poet's lifetime. It is a translation of one poet by one poet, with
constant reference to the Concordance, by which the Frenchman's
lexical practices may be acknowledged if not recovered. Thus to
proceed with a corpus engages the translator in a different atti-
tude—compels a different enterprise—from a rendering of indi-
vidual poems chosen out of that corpus. The emphasis here is not
on the varnish to which a single poem is susceptible, but on the
hope of articulating a sustained structure among all the poems.
Like *Leaves of Grass*, *Les Fleurs du Mal* is a recognizable (if variable)
entity, proposed by the poet as a cumulative whole. Some of the
methods by which the poet arrives at such a unity, such a unison
at least, are not within my reach. The reader will notice that for
the most part I have not sought to make the verses rhyme (where-
as Baudelaire *always* rhymes when he writes in verse). Yet I have
schemed, conscious as I am of the obloquy James Agate once cast
upon a translator of *Cyrano*: "He refuses to rhyme and takes ref-
uge in blank verse, like a tight-rope walker whose wire is stretched
along the floor." My scheming has sought other means of getting
the wire into the air; I have employed all the artifices in my pow-
er to make up for, even to suggest, the consentaneous regularities
that the persistent use of rhyme affords. Here was an occasion, it

seemed to me, when the sacrifice of a minor stratagem to a major one was in order—eschewing "terminal consonance" for the sake of cumulative effects, that "secret architecture" Baudelaire so prided himself upon. Even in the slenderest lyrics, when a rhyming music appears to be the justification for everything—or at least for anything—I have investigated other tactics for keeping the poem suspended; for it has been my study to acknowledge, first of all, a thematics that overshadows and underlies the melos.

His attention to thematics, however compensated for, however blandished, implies the translator's trust in the accessibility of what the poetry is "about"—call it the *mythology* of poetry. And surely the mythology of Baudelaire, like the mythology of Whitman, is as powerful as that of any poetry to be found within the modernity that these two helpless masters have—from our perspective—founded. The adjective formed from his name joins that extreme company—Platonic, Byronic, Rabelaisian, Freudian—of words that suggest a world without our having had to read the writers who have bestowed such qualifiers upon us. To be "Baudelairean" in the fashion of Arthur Symons, a fashion of sensational Satanism, is of course not the same thing as to be "Baudelairean" in that of Robert Lowell, a fashion of convulsive and confessional energy; implied mythologies rather than mere melodies are at variance. But it is in any case the translator's responsibility, and his doom, to engender a notion—the better for being the more conscious—of what the implications might be, though he himself cannot say what they are. Translating the work entire has suggested to me that there are so many more notes to be struck, or at least to be sounded, than my predecessors had intimated. Indeed the *intimate* was the first note that was new to me: a certain *private register*, which Gide compares to Chopin's and which I have tried for in especial.

Throughout, certainly, the undertaking has constrained me to an acknowledgment of the splendor and misery of cities, of bodies, an assent to that vast background of negativity against which finally rises the success of *Les Fleurs du Mal*. If I could not always love my originals, I have endeavored to serve them by an attempt to leave them alone, to get out of their way rather than to domesticate them. Baudelaire's poetry concerns us much more, and much more valuably, by its strangeness than by its familiarity: its authentic relation to us is its remoteness. Wanting to keep Baudelaire, I wanted to keep him at a certain distance.

The *Pléiade* edition of Baudelaire, established and annotated by Yves-Gérard Le Dantec, has been my source. I have attempted to dispense with notes, trusting to the understanding of the translation rather than to its overbearing gloss; in a great poet as in a great nation, to borrow Keats's phrase, "the work of an individual is of so little importance; his pleadings and excuses are so uninteresting; his 'way of life' such a nothing: that a preface seems a sort of impertinent bow to Strangers…." Thus chastened, or charged with the sublimity of his office, the translator eagerly makes way for his poet, proud and humble in the necessary dosages.

I must acknowledge, though with no real effort to repay, some serious debts: to my publisher, David Godine, whose suggestion that I undertake the project has appeared, more often than even he could divine, something like an offer of the last straw, but whose commitment to "our book" has sustained me throughout; to my editor, Sarah Saint-Onge, whose devotion to Baudelaire repeatedly plucked me back from "departures" as from the brink of an abyss; to four friends—a painter, a novelist, two poets—who have read the manuscript through and attempted to save me from many blunders; their counsel has blended into an abiding vigilance that I found indispensable, and I record my fondest gratitude to David Alexander, to Sanford Friedman, and to James Merrill and John Hollander. A word more about the last: Ever since we were in college together, John Hollander's authority in literary matters has been a resource to me, and I remember as a kind of proleptic grace the effect his own translations of Baudelaire, some thirty years ago, had upon my notions of what might be done, or at least not left undone; I hope to have proved worthy of those early and shared intuitions.

I am not certain it is a translator's place to dedicate his efforts to anyone but his original, yet I may say, surely, that this translation has been made during a period of mourning for a friend whose character and achievement continue to remind me of all I cherish, and not only in literary matters; so I inscribe the translation to the memory of Roland Barthes.

Richard Howard
December 1981

A BAUDELAIRE CHRONOLOGY

1819 The widower Joseph-François Baudelaire (61) marries Caroline Archimbaud-Dufaÿs (26).

1821 Charles-Pierre Baudelaire born in Paris on April 9; baptized at Saint-Sulpice, June 7.

1827 Baudelaire's father dies.

1828 Baudelaire's mother marries Captain Jacques Aupick (39).

1832 Baudelaire boards at the Collège de Lyon.

1836 Baudelaire boards at the Lycée Louis-le-Grand in Paris.

1839 Baudelaire is expelled for lack of discipline; completes his studies at the Pension Levêque et Bailly, receives his bachelor's degree.

1841 Baudelaire lives independent of his family in Paris on an inheritance from his father. Distressed by the young man's apparently dissolute existence as well as by his refusal to prepare himself for any other career than that of a writer, the Aupicks send him on a long sea voyage; Baudelaire visits Mauritius and Ile Bourbon (Réunion).

1842 Baudelaire returns to Paris; meets Gautier, Banville; in June he rents a room on the Ile Saint-Louis—the Hashish Club meets in the building; accompanying Nadar to the theater, Baudelaire sees and falls in love with Jeanne Duval, a mulatto actress; he contracts the first of the debts that harass him the rest of his life.

1843 Baudelaire collaborates with Prarond on a project for a play in verse; sends an admiring letter to Sainte-Beuve with a verse epistle; at least fifteen of what were to become *Les Fleurs du Mal* were composed by this time.

1844   Alarmed by her son's increasing improvidence, Mme Aupick appoints Désiré Ancelle as Baudelaire's legal guardian.

1845   Publication of Baudelaire's first signed works—the *Salon of 1845*, a 72-page pamphlet, and the poem "To a Creole Lady" (signed Baudelaire-Dufays). In June, Baudelaire informs Ancelle of his intention to commit suicide after bequeathing all he owns to Jeanne Duval.

1846   Publication of the *Salon of 1846*; on the back of the work is announced the forthcoming publication of *Les Lesbiennes*, a collection of poems by the same author.

1847   Publication of the story *Le Fanfarlo*, after Balzac; Baudelaire falls in love with Marie Daubrun, an actress; the Salon of 1847 rejects Courbet's portrait of Baudelaire.

1848   General Aupick assigned to Constantinople as "Ministre plénipotentiare"; before leaving, he reproaches his stepson for not breaking off with Jeanne Duval. Baudelaire breaks off relations with his mother; during the Revolution of 1848 he is heard to say he intends to shoot General Aupick; later, Baudelaire abandons his revolutionary enthusiasm, to the point of adopting the views of Joseph de Maistre; begins translating Poe; announces the forthcoming publication of a collection of poems to be called *Les Limbes* (Limbo).

1849   Death of Edgar Allan Poe in Baltimore.

1850   Visit to Dijon (probably to escape creditors), joined by Jeanne Duval; secondary symptoms of a syphilitic infection contracted several years before.

1851   Publication of *Du Vin et du haschisch*; also of eleven poems as "Les Limbes," which will appear in *Les Fleurs du Mal*. The Aupicks return from Constantinople, remaining briefly in Paris, where Mme Aupick finds her son living in squalor, then joins her husband in Madrid.

1852   Publication of essay on Poe and further translation; Baudelaire meets and is attracted by Mme Apollonie Sabatier, for whom he writes a number of poems he sends her anonymously; separates from Jeanne Duval, promising always to look after her financial needs but swearing never to see her again.

1853   Baudelaire's physical and intellectual misery increases to the point where he is unable to reply to offers of theater directors who have asked for a libretto and a play. Jeanne Duval is sick and penniless as well. General Aupick is named a senator and returns to Paris. Despite his poverty, Baudelaire assumes expenses for the funeral of Jeanne Duval's mother.

1854   Baudelaire outlines the scenario of a play for the actor Tisserand. His debts increase. He informs his mother he intends to return to Jeanne Duval. Friendship with Barbey d'Aurevilly.

1855   Publication in *La Revue des Deux Mondes* of eighteen poems under the title *Les Fleurs du Mal*, though this title is not Baudelaire's but suggested to him by Hippolyte Babou. Baudelaire writes a letter to George Sand seeking a role for Marie Daubrun; first publication of some of the prose poems.

1856   Publication of a volume of Baudelaire's translations of Poe; Baudelaire signs a contract for a volume of poems entitled *Les Fleurs du Mal* with the publisher and bibliophile Poulet-Malassis. Quarrel with Jeanne Duval and another separation.

1857   Death of Senator Aupick; Mme Aupick retires to Honfleur. Publication of *Les Fleurs du Mal* in an edition of 1,300 copies. The public prosecutor has the edition seized and issues a suit against Baudelaire and his publisher; the court condemns Baudelaire to a fine and orders the removal of six poems ("Lethe," "Jewels," "Lesbos," "Damned Women," "Against Her Levity," "Metamorphoses of the Vampire"); Baudelaire writes his essay on Flaubert, whose novel *Madame Bovary* had been condemned for indecency by the courts that same year; letter from Victor Hugo in Guernsey, praising *Les Fleurs du Mal*.

1858　Baudelaire's health extremely bad; urged by his mother to do so, he considers joining her in Honfleur, and makes two visits to her there; the Minister of Public Education awards Baudelaire a grant for his Poe translations; the fine for Les Fleurs du Mal is reduced; despite many quarrels, Baudelaire lives with Jeanne Duval; friendship with his publisher Poulet-Malassis increases, and Baudelaire spends two weeks as his guest at Alençon.

1859　Baudelaire sends "Travelers" (*Le Voyage*) to Maxime Du Camp with a dedication; publication of essay on Gautier as a pamphlet with a prefatory letter from Hugo (..."*un frisson nouveau*").

1860　New contract with Poulet-Malassis for a second edition of *Les Fleurs du Mal*; publication of *Les Paradis artificiels* and *Curiosités esthétiques*, as well as of what was to become *l'Art romantique*; Baudelaire suffers a minor cerebral stroke; writes essay on De Quincey, who has just died; moves into a Neuilly apartment, which he shares with Jeanne Duval.

1861　Publication of essay on Wagner; decides to write (and publish) *Mon cœur mis à nu*; decides to offer his candidacy for the Académie Française—discouraged from doing so by Sainte-Beuve; leaves the Neuilly apartment after quarrels with Jeanne Duval's "brother"; publication of the second edition of *Les Fleurs du Mal* with thirty-five new poems, an edition of 1,500 copies; new syphilitic symptoms; Baudelaire's finances reach a new low; Jeanne Duval is hospitalized; Baudelaire publishes his essay on Victor Hugo.

1862　Baudelaire signs contract for a third edition of *Les Fleurs du Mal*, though this comes to nothing, Poulet-Malassis having to flee to Brussels on account of bankruptcy; publication of Swinburne's enthusiastic essay on *Les Fleurs du Mal* in *The Spectator*; Baudelaire publishes an essay praising Whistler and Manet.

1863   Publication of Baudelaire's essay on Delacroix, who has just died, and of his essay on Constantin Guys; visit to Belgium.

1864   Baudelaire attempts to establish residence in Brussels, but his lectures there are a failure; his health and financial situation worsen.

1866   Publication of essays on Baudelaire by Mallarmé (23) and Verlaine (21). *Nouvelles Fleurs du Mal,* sixteen poems posterior to the second edition, published in Catulle Mendès's *Parnasse Contemporain*; Baudelaire's health worsens—his aphasia is almost complete—and he is hospitalized in Brussels; Mme Aupick arrives there, and with Poulet-Malassis takes the mute and half-paralyzed poet for drives around the city; Poulet-Malassis publishes 260 copies of *Epaves* (Wreckage), a pamphlet of twenty-three poems including the six condemned by the French courts; Baudelaire returns to Paris with his mother and is hospitalized in the sanatorium of Dr Duval, where he receives visits from Sainte-Beuve, Maxime Du Camp, Banville, Leconte de Lisle, Nadar, and Mme Paul Meurice, who plays Wagner to him on the piano.

1867   After months of suffering, Baudelaire asks for the sacraments, and dies (46) in his mother's arms. Baudelaire is buried in the cemetery of Montparnasse, beside General Aupick.

1868   Publication of Baudelaire's works, including the third edition of *Les Fleurs du Mal* and, the following year, *Le Spleen de Paris*.

1870   Nadar glimpses Jeanne Duval in the streets of Paris—the last knowledge we have of her.

1871   Death of Mme Aupick in Honfleur (78).

1887   Publication of posthumous works, correspondence, *Fusées*, and *Mon Cœur mis à nu*.

DISCUSSIONS OF BAUDELAIRE
SIGNIFICANT TO THE TRANSLATION

Erich Auerbach | *"The Aesthetic Dignity of Les Fleurs du Mal,"* in *Scenes from the Drama of European Literature*, 1959.

Roland Barthes | "Baudelaire's Theatre," in *Critical Essays*, 1972.

Georges Bataille | "Baudelaire," in *La Littérature et le Mal*, 1957.

Walter Benjamin | "The Task of the Translator," "On Some Motifs in Baudelaire," in *Illuminations*, 1969; *CB: A Lyric Poet in the Era of High Capitalism*, 1973.

Leo Bersani | *Baudelaire and Freud*, 1977.

Maurice Blanchot | "Une édition des *Fleurs du Mal*," in *Faux Pas*, 1943; "L'Echec de Baudelaire," in *La Part du Feu*, 1949.

Yves Bonnefoy | "Les Fleurs du Mal," in *L'Improbable*, 1959.

Michel Butor | *Histoire Extraordinaire, Essay on a Dream of Baudelaire's*, 1969.

R. T. Cargo | *Concordance to Baudelaire's* Les Fleurs du Mal, 1965.

T. S. Eliot | "Baudelaire," in *Selected Essays*, 1930.

Pierre Emmanuel | *Baudelaire, The Paradox of Redemptive Satanism*, 1967.

Hugo Friedrich | "Baudelaire," in *The Structure of Modern Poetry*, 1974.

André Gide   "Baudelaire et M. Faguet," in
                                    Nouveaux Prétextes, 1921; "Préface
                                    aux *Fleurs du Mal*," in *Incidences*, 1924.

Pierre-Jean Jouve   *Tombeau de Baudelaire*, 1958.

Reinhard Kuhn   *The Demon of Noontide*, 1976.

Claude-Edmonde Magny   "Ce Grand Bélier: Baudelaire," in
                                    Littérature et Critique, 1971.

Marcel Proust   "Sainte-Beuve et Baudelaire,"
                                    "Apropos de Baudelaire," in *Contre
                                    Sainte-Beuve*, 1971.

Jean-Pierre Richard   "Profondeur de Baudelaire," in *Poésie
                                    et Profondeur*, 1955.

Jean-Paul Sartre   *Baudelaire*, 1947.

Pierre Schneider   "Baudelaire, Poète de la
                                    Fragmentation," in *La Voix vive*, 1953.

Enid Starkie   *Baudelaire*, 1958.

Martin Turnell   *Baudelaire: A Study of His Poetry*, 1972.

Paul Valéry   "Situation de Baudelaire," in *Variété
                                    II*, 1930.

to the impeccable poet
to the perfect magician of French letters
to my beloved and revered master & friend
Théophile Gautier
with a sense of the deepest humility
I dedicate these sickly flowers

C.B.

THE FLOWERS OF EVIL

The Flowers of Evil

TO THE READER

Stupidity, delusion, selfishness and lust
torment our bodies and possess our minds,
and we sustain our affable remorse
the way a beggar nourishes his lice.

Our sins are stubborn, our contrition lame;
we want our scruples to be worth our while—
how cheerfully we crawl back to the mire:
a few cheap tears will wash our stains away!

Satan Trismegistus subtly rocks
our ravished spirits on his wicked bed
until the precious metal of our will
is leached out by this cunning alchemist:

the Devil's hand directs our every move—
the things we loathed become the things we love;
day by day we drop through stinking shades
quite undeterred on our descent to Hell.

Like a poor profligate who sucks and bites
the withered breast of some well-seasoned trull,
we snatch in passing at clandestine joys
and squeeze the oldest orange harder yet.

Wriggling in our brains like a million worms,
a demon demos holds its revels there,
and when we breathe, the Lethe in our lungs
trickles sighing on its secret course.

If rape and arson, poison and the knife
have not yet stitched their ludicrous designs

3

onto the banal buckram of our fates,
it is because our souls lack enterprise!

But here among the scorpions and the hounds,
the jackals, apes and vultures, snakes and wolves,
monsters that howl and growl and squeal and crawl,
in all the squalid zoo of vices, one

is even uglier and fouler than the rest,
although the least flamboyant of the lot;
this beast would gladly undermine the earth
and swallow all creation in a yawn;

I speak of Boredom which with ready tears
dreams of hangings as it puffs its pipe.
Reader, you know this squeamish monster well,
—hypocrite reader,—my alias,—my twin!

SPLEEN AND IDEAL

1 ❋ CONSECRATION

When by an edict of the sovereign powers
the Poet enters this indifferent world,
his mother, spurred to blasphemy by shame,
clenches her fists at a condoling God:

"Why not have given me a brood of snakes
rather than make me rear this laughing-stock?
I curse the paltry pleasures of the night
on which my womb conceived my punishment!

Since I am chosen out of all my sex
to bring this scandal to my bed and board,
and since I cannot toss the stunted freak,
as if he were a love-letter, into the fire,

at least I can transfer Your hate to him,
the instrument of all Your wickedness,
and so torment this miserable tree
that not one of its blighted buds will grow!"

Choking on her enmity, and blind
to operations of the eternal plan,
she readies in a Gehenna of her own
the torture-chamber of a mother's crimes.

Yet under an Angel's unseen tutelage
the outcast child, enchanted by the sun,
will recognize in all he eats and drinks
golden ambrosia and nectar of the gods.

With winds for playmate and with clouds for nurse,
he sings the very stations of his cross—
the Spirit who attends his pilgrimage
weeps to see him happy as a bird.

Those he longs to love give him wide berth,
or, since he offers no resistance, vie
to be the first to make him moan with pain,
testing their violence, one after the next.

Fouling the food that he is meant to taste,
they spit in his wine, mix ashes in his bread,
whatever he touches they declare unclean
and claim they fear to walk where he has been.

Meanwhile his wife, in public places, cries:
"Since he believes me worthy to adore,
I'll deal in worship as old idols did
and, like them, have myself touched up with gold;

why not? I'll glut myself with frankincense
and genuflections, gifts of meat and wine—
we'll see if in so reverent a heart
my smile usurps the honor of the gods!

and when I weary of these impious tricks
the time will come for a laying-on of hands:
these frail and adamant hands, these harpies' nails
will claw their way into his waiting breast;

as if a sparrow trembled in my fist
I'll tear his beating heart out of his flesh
and toss it underfoot disdainfully
to make a mouthful for my favorite pet!"

To Heaven where he sees a splendid throne
the oblivious Poet lifts his pious arms,
and blinding flashes of his intellect
keep him from noticing the angry mob:

"Thanks be to God, Who gives us suffering
as sacred remedy for all our sins,

that best and purest essence which prepares
the strong in spirit for divine delights!

I know the Poet has a place apart
among the holy legions' blessed ranks;
You will invite him to the eternal feast
of Dominations, Virtues, Thrones and Powers:

I know that pain is the one nobility
upon which Hell itself cannot encroach;
that if I am to weave my mystic crown
I must braid into it all time, all space . . .

But even the lost gems of ancient Palmyra,
metals sunk in the earth, pearls in the sea,
set by Your hand, could not approximate
the brightness of this perfect diadem!

for it will be made of nothing but pure light
drawn from the hallowed hearth of primal rays,
of which our mortal eyes, for all their might,
are only a mournful mirror, a darkened glass."

2 ❀   THE ALBATROSS

Often, to pass the time on board, the crew
will catch an albatross, one of those big birds
that nonchalantly chaperone a ship
across the bitter fathoms of the sea.

Tied to the deck, this sovereign of space,
as if embarrassed by its clumsiness,
pitiably lets its great white wings
drag at its sides like a pair of unshipped oars.

How weak and awkward, even comical
this traveler but lately so adroit—

9

one deckhand sticks a pipestem in its beak,
another mocks the cripple that once flew!

The Poet is like this monarch of the clouds
riding the storm above the marksman's range;
exiled on the ground, hooted and jeered,
he cannot walk because of his great wings.

3 ❋   ELEVATION

Above the lake in the valley and the grove
along the hillside, high over the sea
and the passing clouds, and even past the sun!
to the farthest confines of the starry vault

mount, my spirit, wander at your ease
and range exultant through transparent space
like a rugged swimmer reveling in the waves
with an unutterable male delight.

Ascend beyond the sickly atmosphere
to a higher plane, and purify yourself
by drinking as if it were ambrosia
the fire that fills and fuels Emptiness.

Free from the futile strivings and the cares
which dim existence to a realm of mist,
happy is he who wings an upward way
on mighty pinions to the fields of light;

whose thoughts like larks spontaneously rise
into the morning sky; whose flight, unchecked,
outreaches life and readily comprehends
the language of flowers and of all mute things.

4 ❋ CORRESPONDENCES

The pillars of Nature's temple are alive
and sometimes yield perplexing messages;
forests of symbols between us and the shrine
remark our passage with accustomed eyes.

Like long-held echoes, blending somewhere else
into one deep and shadowy unison
as limitless as darkness and as day,
the sounds, the scents, the colors correspond.

There are odors succulent as young flesh,
sweet as flutes, and green as any grass,
while others—rich, corrupt and masterful—

possess the power of such infinite things
as incense, amber, benjamin and musk,
to praise the senses' raptures and the mind's.

5 ❋ "I PRIZE THE MEMORY..."

I prize the memory of naked ages when
Apollo relished gilding marble limbs
whose agile-fleshed originals achieved
their ecstasy with neither fraud nor fear
and, nursed by that companionable sky,
enjoyed the health of a sublime machine.
Cybele then, abundant in her yield,
did not regard her sons as burdensome,
but, tender-hearted she-wolf, graciously
suckled the universe at her brown dugs.
Lithe and powerful, a man deserved
his pride in beauties who called him their king—
flawless fruit engendered without shame,
whose ripened flesh asked only to be tried!

Today the poet eager to recall
such human splendor, visiting the sites
where men and women show their nakedness,
must feel a cold revulsion in his soul
at the display of flesh he contemplates.
How these deformities cry out for clothes!
—wretched bodies, regular grotesques,
runty, paunchy, flabby, scrawny, lame,
brats whom Utility, a pitiless god,
has swaddled in his brazen diapers!
Look at the women—pale as tallow, gnawed
and nourished by debauch—the girls who bear
the burden of their mothers' vice or wear
the hideous stigmas of fecundity!

True, in our corruption we possess
beauties unrevealed to ancient times:
countenances cankered by the heart
and, so to speak, the charm of listlessness;
but subtle though they are, such artifacts
of a belated muse will never keep
our sickly race from offering to youth
its truest homage; youth we worship still,
its frank expression, its untroubled brow,
its eyes as bright as water; sacred youth
that shares—unconscious as a singing bird,
a flower, or the blue sky's radiance—
its song, its scent, its irresistible warmth!

6 ❋ GUIDING LIGHTS

Rubens
Garden of Sloth, Lethe's fountainhead,
pillow of flesh where no dream is of love
but where life seethes and surges endlessly
like wind in heaven, sea within the sea;

Leonardo
A mirror somber in its distances
where charming angels with a mysterious
gentle smile appear beneath the shade
of pines and glaciers which enclose their realm;

Rembrandt
Sorry hospital echoing with sighs,
adorned by one enormous crucifix,
where tearful prayers rise from excrement
and a sudden ray of winter sunlight falls;

Michelangelo
No man's land where every Hercules
becomes a Christ, where mighty phantoms rise
bolt upright from their graves and in the gloom
rend their shrouds by reaching out their hands;

Puget
Faun's impudence and a prize-fighter's rage,
jaundiced and weak, your great heart gorged with pride
that you could find the beauty in their crimes—
you, the convicts' melancholy emperor;

Watteau
Festivities where many famous hearts
flutter like moths as they go up in flame,
the chandeliers in this enchanted glade
cast a madness on the minuet;

Goya
Nightmare crammed with unfathomable things,
witches roasting fetuses in a pan,
crones at a mirror served by naked girls
who straighten stockings to entice the Fiend;

Delacroix
Evil angels haunt this lake of blood
darkened by the green shade of the firs,
where under a stricken sky the trumpet-calls
like a fanfare by Weber fade away . . .

These blasphemies, these ecstasies, these cries,
these groans and curses, tears and *Te Deums*,
re-echo through a thousand labyrinths—
a holy opium for mortal hearts!

A thousand sentries pass the order on,
a cry repeated by a thousand messengers;
hunters shout it, lost in the deep woods;
the beacon flares on a thousand citadels!

This, O Lord, is the best evidence
that we can offer of our dignity,
this sob that swells from age to age and dies
out on the shore of Your eternity!

7 ❋   THE SICK MUSE

Good morning, Muse—what's wrong? Something you saw
        last night is left in your hollow eyes;
        your color's bad, your cheeks are cold
with horror, with madness!—and you don't say a word.

Are you silenced by the love and fear dispensed
        by greenish vampires, rosy ghouls?
        Or sunk in some legendary bog,
held under by nightmare's unrelenting fist?

Not like this . . . I want you safe and sound,
        thinking fit thoughts, breathing deep,
        your Christian bloodstream coursing strong

and steadfast as the copious Classical vein
in the double realm of Pan and Apollo—
Lord of the Harvest, Father of Song.

8 ❋ THE MUSE FOR HIRE

My palace-loving Muse, can you afford—
once January launches out of the North
night after night of desolating snow—
the coals to comfort your frostbitten feet?

Are streetlamps through your shutters stove enough
to make your huddled shoulders warm again?
When your belly is as empty as your purse,
what will you do—harvest the stars for gold?

Try other ways to earn your nightly bread:
suppose you swing a censer (just for show)
and like a choirboy mumble all the hymns;

or, naked as an acrobat, reveal
laughing charms so wet with secret tears
they rouse the tired businessman to pay.

9 ❋ THE BAD MONK

There was a time when all refectory walls
were frescoed with the images of Truth
whose influence, kindling pious appetite,
tempered the chill of their austerity.

Christ was the Master then, and more than one
illustrious (and unremembered) monk
would scour the cemetery for his theme
and for his models, glorifying Death.

My habitation for eternity
is standing bare, the tomb that is my soul—
I haunt the naked walls of this sad place...

O slothful cenobite! When shall I make
the living pageant of my misery
into the work of my hands and the love of my eyes?

10 ✱ THE ENEMY

My youth was nothing but a lowering storm
occasionally lanced by sudden suns;
torrential rains have done their work so well
that no fruit ripens in my garden now.

Already the autumn of ideas has come,
and I must dig and rake and dig again
if I am to reclaim the flooded soil
collapsing into holes the size of graves.

I dream of new flowers, but who can tell
if this eroded swamp of mine affords
the mystic nourishment on which they thrive ...

Time consumes existence pain by pain,
and the hidden enemy that gnaws our heart
feeds on the blood we lose, and flourishes!

11 ✱ ARTIST UNKNOWN

Flesh is willing, but the Soul requires
    Sisyphean patience for its song.
Time, Hippocrates remarked, is short
    and Art is long.

No illustrious tombstones ornament
        the lonely churchyard where I often go
to hear my heart, a muffled drum, parade
            incognito.

"Many a gem," the poet mourns, abides
        forgotten in the dust,
            unnoticed there;

"many a rose" regretfully confides
        the secret of its scent
            to empty air.

12 ❀ PREVIOUS EXISTENCE

I lived a long time under vast porticoes
whose splendors altered with the sea all day;
by evening their majestic pillars turned,
row after row, into tall basalt caves.

Solemn and magical the waves rolled in
bearing images of heaven on the swell,
blending the sovereign music that they made
with sunset colors mirrored in my eyes.

There I lived, in a rapture of repose,
amid the glories of that sky, that sea,
and I had naked slaves, perfumed with musk,

to fan me by the hour with rustling fronds,
and their one study was to diagnose
the secret torment which had sickened me.

13 ❀ GYPSIES ON THE ROAD

The prophet-tribe with burning eyes set out
yesterday, women bearing on their backs
brats whose clamorous greed is satisfied
by offering an ever-ready dug;

beside a wagon sheltering their brood
the men trudge, shouldering their oily guns
and gazing nowhere, eyelids heavier
for having lost their castles in the air.

The cricket hidden in its sandy lair
sings all the louder as they pass;
a favoring Goddess makes the desert bloom,

and where they wander springs transform the rock,
these vagabonds in front of whom unfurl
familiar empires of oncoming night.

14 ❀ MAN AND SEA

Man—a free man—always loves the sea
and in its endlessly unrolling surge
will contemplate his soul as in a glass
where gulfs as bitter gape within his mind.

Into this image of himself he dives,
his arms and eyes wide open and his heart
sometimes diverted from its own dead march
by the tides of that untamable complaint.

How grim their combat, and yet how discreet
—who has sounded to its depths the human heart?
and who has plucked its riches from the sea?—
so jealously they guard their secrets, both!

Countless the ages past and still to come
in which they wage their unrelenting war
for sheer delight in carnage and in death,
implacable brothers and eternal foes!

15 ✶ IMPENITENT

When Don Juan went down to that last river
  and had given Charon his coin,
a grim beggar proud as the first Cynic
  vengefully rowed him across.

Women parading their fallen breasts
  writhed in the darkness behind him,
and their moans faded like the lowing
  of cattle led to slaughter.

Grinning, Sganarelle demanded his pay,
  while Don Luis, in a fury,
cursed from the shades lining the shore
  a son who mocked his father.

Veiled and trembling, Elvira beckoned
  the false husband—the lover!—
imploring repeatedly one last smile
  sweet as his first promise.

Huge in armor the Stone Guest towered
  at the prow where the stream divided;
but over his sword the hero stared at the wake
  and calmly ignored them all.

16 ✸ THE PUNISHMENT OF PRIDE

Once upon a time, in the wondrous age
of theological splendors, runs the tale,
one of the greatest Doctors of the Church,
having wakened many slumbering hearts
and plumbed them to their pandemonic depths,
having risen to celestial heights
by ways unheard of, even to himself,
where only the Pure in Spirit can have climbed—
this man, as one above himself and moved
to panic by Satanic pride, exclaimed:
"Little Jesus! I have raised Thee up;
yet had I sought to pierce Thy armor's chink,
Thy shame would be the equal of Thy fame,
and Thou no more than a vile homunculus!"

Upon the instant, Reason's light went out
and darkness shrouded this once-searching mind;
Chaos made her shrine within a skull
which once had been a living temple filled
with opulence and ceremonial speech!
Night and silence were its tenants now,
as in a cellar when the key is lost.
Henceforth he was no more than an animal,
knowing neither season, day, nor hour,
and when he stumbled blindly through the fields,
filthy and futile as a worn-out thing,
the children laughed and chased him, throwing stones.

17 ✸ BEAUTY

Conceive me as a dream of stone:
my breast, where mortals come to grief,
is made to prompt all poets' love,
mute and noble as matter itself.

With snow for flesh, with ice for heart,
I sit on high, an unguessed sphinx
begrudging acts that alter forms;
I never laugh—and never weep.

In studious awe the poets brood
before my monumental pose
aped from the proudest pedestal,

and to bind these docile lovers fast
I freeze the world in a perfect mirror:
the timeless light of my wide eyes.

18 ❀ **THE IDEAL**

My heart is closed to belles in curlicues,
those worshipped beauties of a shopworn age
when fingers were for spinets and when feet
wore out six pairs of silver-buckled shoes.

I leave to Gavarni, anemia's laureate,
his twittering flock of insubstantial girls—
in all those sallow blossoms who could find
one rose to reconcile my red ideal?

This heart is cavernous and it requires
Lady Macbeth and an aptitude for crime,
some Aeschylean flower of the South,

or Michelangelo's great daughter, Night,
who slumbrously contorts the marble charms
he carved to satiate a titan's mouth.

19 ❀   GIANTESS

Had I been there when primal Nature teemed
with monstrous progeny, I would have tried
to live beside some mammoth girl, the way
a cat will sprawl at the feet of a queen;

loving to watch her ripen (body and soul
growing tremendous with her terrible games),
to guess from rainclouds darkening her eyes
what thunderbolts were gathered in her heart;

scaling the slopes of her enormous knees,
to saunter through the landscape of her lap,
and when the fetid summers made her stretch

herself across the countryside, to sleep
untroubled in the shadow of her breasts
like a peaceful village at the mountain's base.

20 ❀   JEWELS

My darling was naked, or nearly, for knowing my heart
she had left on her jewels, the bangles and chains
whose jingling music gave her the conquering air
of a Moorish slave on days her master is pleased.

Whenever I hear such insolent harmonies,
that scintillating world of metal and stone
beguiles me altogether, and I am enthralled
by objects whose sound is a synonym for light.

For there she lay on the couch, allowing herself
to be adored, a secret smile indulging
the deep and tenacious currents of my love
which rose against her body like a tide.

Eyes fixed on mine with the speculative glare
of a half-tamed tiger, she kept altering poses,
and the incorporation of candor into lust
gave new charms to her metamorphoses;

calmly I watched, with a certain detachment at first,
as the swanlike arms uncoiled, and then the legs,
the sleek thighs shifting, shiny as oil,
the belly, the breasts—that fruit on my vine—

clustered, more tempting than wicked cherubim,
to undermine what peace I had achieved,
dislodging my soul from its rock-crystal throne
of contemplation, once so aloof, so serene.

As if a new Genesis had been at work,
I saw a boy's torso joined to Antiope's hips,
belying that lithe waist by those wide loins . . .
O the pride of rouge upon that tawny skin!

And then, the lamp having given up the ghost,
the dying coals made the only light in the room:
each time they heaved another flamboyant sigh,
they flushed that amber-colored flesh with blood!

21 ❀ THE MASK

ALLEGORICAL STATUE IN THE STYLE OF THE
RENAISSANCE

It is a legacy of Tuscan skill;
in ripples of her surging musculature
see how the holy sisters, Power and Grace,
sustain this woman's beauty in a form
so faultless as to seem miraculous—
taking pride of place above rich beds
to charm a prince's leisure, or a pope's...

Notice the faint voluptuous smile that shows,
that *shares*, the consummation of Desire;
observe that teasing glance which penetrates
the subtle coquetry of gauzy veils
around a face whose every feature speaks,
not just the parted lips too shy to boast:
"When Lust commands me, even Love obeys!"
Look how the languor in her posture adds
a sweet submission to such majesty;
come closer—walk around her loveliness...

What blasphemy of art is this! Upon
a body made to offer every bliss
appear...two heads! Some kind of monster? No—

one is merely a mask—a grinning cheat
this smile articulated so cunningly!
Look there: contorted in her misery,
the actual head, the woman's countenance
lost in the shadow of the lying mask...
Pathos of true beauty! the bright tears
trickle into my astonished heart;
your lie intoxicates me, and my soul
slakes its passion in your brimming eyes!

—Why is she weeping? Surely such a face
would put all mankind, vanquished, at her feet!
What secret evil feeds on her firm flesh?

—She weeps, you fool, for having lived! and for
living—yet what she laments the most,
what makes her body tremble head to toe,
is that tomorrow she will have to live,
and all tomorrows after—like ourselves!

22 ❋ HYMN TO BEAUTY

Do you come from on high or out of the abyss,
O Beauty? Godless yet divine, your gaze
indifferently showers favor and shame,
and therefore some have likened you to wine.

Your eyes reflect the sunset and the dawn;
you scatter perfumes like a windy night;
your kisses are a drug, your mouth the urn
dispensing fear to heroes, fervor to boys.

Whether spawned by hell or sprung from the stars,
Fate like a spaniel follows at your heel;
you sow haphazard fortune and despair,
ruling all things, responsible for none.

You walk on corpses, Beauty, undismayed,
and Horror coruscates among your gems;
Murder, one of your dearest trinkets, throbs
on your shameless belly: make it dance!

Dazzled, the dayfly flutters round your wick,
crackles, flares, and cries: I bless this torch!
The pining lover for his lady swoons
like a dying man adoring his own tomb.

Who cares if you come from paradise or hell,
appalling Beauty, artless and monstrous scourge,
if only your eyes, your smile or your foot reveal
the Infinite I love and have never known?

Come from Satan, come from God—who cares,
Angel or Siren, rhythm, fragrance, light,
provided you transform—O my one queen!
this hideous universe, this heavy hour?

23 ❋   BY ASSOCIATION

These warm fall nights I breathe, eyes closed, the scent
of your welcoming breasts, and thereupon appears
the coast of maybe Malabar—some paradise
besotted by the sun's monotonous fire;

an idle isle where Nature grants to men
with bodies slim and strong, to women who
meet your eye with amazing willingness,
the rarest trees, the ripest fruit; and then,

guided by your fragrance to enchanted ground,
I glimpse a harbor filled with masts and sails
still troubled by the slow-receding tide,

while the aroma of green tamarinds
dilates my nostrils as it drifts to sea
and mingles in my soul with the sailors' song.

24 ❋   THE HEAD OF HAIR

Ecstatic fleece that ripples to your nape
and reeks of negligence in every curl!
To people my dim cubicle tonight
with memories shrouded in that head of hair,
I'd have it flutter like a handkerchief!

For torpid Asia, torrid Africa
—the wilderness I thought a world away—
survive at the heart of this dark continent...
As other souls set sail to music, mine,
O my love! embarks on your redolent hair.

Take me, tousled current, to where men
as mighty as the trees they live among

submit like them to the sun's long tyranny;
ebony sea, you bear a brilliant dream
of sails and pennants, mariners and masts,

a harbor where my soul can slake its thirst
for color, sound and smell—where ships that glide
among the seas of golden silk throw wide
their yardarms to embrace a glorious sky
palpitating in eternal heat.

Drunk, and in love with drunkenness, I'll dive
into this ocean where the other lurks,
and solaced by these waves, my restlessness
will find a fruitful lethargy at last,
rocking forever at aromatic ease.

Blue hair, vault of shadows, be for me
the canopy of overarching sky;
here at the downy roots of every strand
I stupefy myself on the mingled scent
of musk and tar and coconut oil for hours...

For hours? Forever! Into that splendid mane
let me braid rubies, ropes of pearls to bind
you indissolubly to my desire—
you the oasis where I dream, the gourd
from which I gulp the wine of memory.

25 ❀ "URN OF STILLED SORROWS..."

Urn of stilled sorrows, I worship you
as if you were the dome of night itself,
and all the more because you turn away
and seem, for setting off my darkness, more
mockingly to magnify the space
which bars me from those blue immensities.

I lay my siege, advance to the attack
like worms that congregate around a corpse,
and prize that cold disdain, O cruel beast,
that makes you even lovelier to me!

26 * "YOU'D SLEEP WITH ANYONE..."

You'd sleep with anyone at all, you slut!
(A clue to just how bored you are and just
how brutal boredom makes your soul.) To keep
your teeth incisive for this singular sport,
you claim a daily ration of . . . fresh hearts!
Your eyes, lit up like shops to lure their trade
or fireworks in the park on holidays,
insolently make use of borrowed power
and never learn (you might say, "in the dark")
what law it is that governs their *good looks*.

Blind and unfeeling instrument of pain,
my salutary leech, how could you fail
to see in every mirror that you pass
your "charms" go pale if not quite blank with shame . . .
How could you help wincing at the scope
of all the knowing harm you perpetrate
when Nature, noted for mighty subterfuge,
avails herself of you, My Queen of Sins
—of you, vile animal!—to breed a genius?
O squalid dignity . . . Sublime disgrace!

27 * SED NON SATIATA

Daughter of darkness, slattern deity
rank with musk and nicotine, the spawn
of filthy covens or a shaman's rites,
ebony fetish, nameless talisman...And yet

to wine, to opium even, I prefer
the elixir of your lips on which love flaunts
itself; and in the wasteland of desire
your eyes afford the wells to slake my thirst.

Seal them, those sooty holes from which your soul
rains hellfire too, relentless sorceress!
I am no Styx, to cradle you nine times,

alas! and cannot with some Fury's lust,
to break your spirit and your heart, become
in your bed's inferno . . . Persephone!

28 ❀   "EVEN WHEN SHE WALKS..."

Even when she walks she seems to dance!
Her garments writhe and glisten like long snakes
obedient to the rhythm of the wands
by which a fakir wakens them to grace.

Like both the desert and the desert sky
insensible to human suffering,
and like the ocean's endless labyrinth
she shows her body with indifference.

Precious minerals form her polished eyes,
and in her strange symbolic nature where
angel and sphinx unite, where diamond,

gold, and steel dissolve into one light,
shines forever, useless as a star,
the sterile woman's icy majesty.

29 ✸ AS IF A SERPENT DANCED

Dear indolent! I love to see
    with every move you make
the iridescence of your skin
    gleam like watered silk.

On your resilient head of hair,
    unfathomable sea
of acrid curls that veer from brown
    to blue inconstancies,

my dreamy soul weighs anchor, sails
    for undiscovered skies
like a galleon in the morning watch
    under a freshening wind.

Cruel? Kind? Your eyes reveal
    nothing but themselves:
cold as a pair of brooches made
    of gold inlaid with steel.

And when you walk to cadences
    of sinuous nonchalance,

it looks as if a serpent danced
    in rhythm to a wand.

Under the burden of your sloth,
    your head—just like a child's—
lolls with all the wobbly grace
    of a baby elephant;

your body lists and rights itself
    like a clipper in high seas,
rolling from side to side until
    the spray has soaked its spars.

And like a current swollen by
  the melt of clashing ice,
when the saliva in your mouth
  surges through your teeth,

I seem to drink a devil's brew,
  salt and sovereign,
as if the sky had liquefied
  and strewn my heart with stars!

30 ❀   CARRION

Remember, my soul, the thing we saw
  that lovely summer day?
On a pile of stones where the path turned off,
  the hideous carrion—

legs in the air, like a whore—displayed,
  indifferent to the last,
a belly slick with lethal sweat
  and swollen with foul gas.

The sun lit up that rottenness
  as though to roast it through,
restoring to Nature a hundredfold
  what she had here made one.

And heaven watched the splendid corpse
  like a flower open wide—
you nearly fainted dead away
  at the perfume it gave off.

Flies kept humming over the guts
  from which a gleaming clot
of maggots poured to finish off
  what scraps of flesh remained.

The tide of trembling vermin sank,
 then bubbled up afresh
as if the carcass, drawing breath,
 by *their* lives lived again

and made a curious music there—
 like running water, or wind,
or the rattle of chaff the winnower
 loosens in his fan.

Shapeless—nothing was left but a dream
 the artist had sketched in,
forgotten, and only later on
 finished from memory.

Behind the rocks an anxious bitch
 eyed us reproachfully,
waiting for the chance to resume
 her interrupted feast.

—Yet you will come to this offence,
 this horrible decay,
you, the light of my life, the sun
 and moon and stars of my love!

Yes, you will come to this, my queen,
 after the sacraments,
when you rot underground among
 the bones already there.

But as their kisses eat you up,
 my Beauty, tell the worms
I've kept the sacred essence, saved
 the form of my rotted loves!

31 ✳ DE PROFUNDIS CLAMAVI

I beg Your mercy—You, the One I Love!
Out of the depths my heart has plumbed, I cry—
the skies are lead, and no horizon pales:
I share this night with blasphemy and dread.

A frozen sun hangs overhead six months;
the other six, the earth is in its shroud—
no trees, no water, not one creature here,
a wasteland naked as the polar north!

Of all the abominations none
is half so cruel as that sun of ice
and darkness worthy of old Chaos itself;

I envy the lot of the lowest animal
that can surrender to a stupid sleep—
so slowly does the skein of time unwind!

32 ✳ THE VAMPIRE

Sudden as a knife you thrust
     into my sorry heart
and strong as a host of demons came,
     gaudy and libertine,

to make in my corrupted mind
     your bed and bedlam there;
—Beast, who bind me to you close
     as convict to his chains,

as gambler to his winning streak,
     as drunkard to his wine,
close as the carrion to its worms—
     I curse you! Be accursed!

I begged the sword by one swift stroke
    to grant me liberty;
nor did my cowardice disdain
    less clear-cut remedies.

Poison and steel, as with one voice,
    contemptuously refused:
"You are not worthy to be free
    of your enslavement, fool!

Suppose we saved you, even now,
    from her supremacy—
your kisses would resuscitate
    your vampire's waiting corpse!"

33 ✸ LETHE

Sullen, lazy beast! creep close
until you lie upon my heart;
I want to fill my trembling hands
with your impenetrable mane,

to soothe my headache in the reek
of you that permeates your skirts
and relish, like decaying flowers,
the redolence of my late love.

In drowsiness sweet as death itself
let my insistent kisses cloud
the gleaming copper of your skin.
I want to sleep—not live, but sleep!

For nothing silences my sobs
like the abyss that is your bed:
oblivion occupies your mouth
and Lethe runs between your lips...

My destiny is my desire
which I obey as if foredoomed:
innocent martyr, eager prey
whose fervor hones his agony;

hemlock is sweet, nepenthe kind—
I'll suck enough to drown my spite
at those entrancing pointed breasts
which never have confined a heart.

34 ❋ "I Spent the Night..."

I spent the night with a gruesome Jewish whore,
and lying there, a corpse beside a corpse,
I fell to dreaming, close to that hired flesh,
of the sad beauty desire denies itself.

I conjured up her natural majesty,
the energy and grace that arm her glance,
the perfumed helmet that her hair creates,
whose memory wakens me to love once more...

O to have idolized that noble flesh,
and from your marble feet to your black mane
to have squandered all the kisses I had saved!

If only by a single easy tear
some night you would consent, my cruel queen,
to dim the splendor of those icy eyes.

35 ❋ Posthumous Regret

The time will come when your dark loveliness
must sleep alone beneath a marble slab

and keep no couch or canopy but this:
a rainy graveyard and a seeping pit.

and when the tombstone overrides your breast
and thighs that once were lithe with unconcern
—denying your heart its rhythms of desire,
your feet the primrose path they used to race—

the Grave, to which I tell my infinite dream
(for graves will always have the poet's trust)
on those high nights when sleep is held in scorn

will ask: "What help is it to you, vain whore,
not to have known what it is the Dead lament?"
And worms will gnaw your flesh, like a regret.

36 ❀ THE CAT

Come here, kitty—sheathe your claws!
    Lie on my loving heart
and let me sink into your eyes
    of agate fused with steel.

When my fingers freely caress
    your head and supple spine,
and my hand thrills to the touch
    of your electric fur,

my mistress comes to mind. Her gaze—
    cold and deep as yours,
my pet—is like a stab of pain,

    and from head to heels
a subtle scent, a dangerous perfume,
    rises from her brown flesh.

37 ❋ DUELLUM

Two warriors have engaged in combat: swords
flash and clash together; blood is spilled.
Such passages of arms are the result
of love in its early phase, a loud pursuit.

The blades are broken—like our youth, my dear:
no more than teeth and nails, discreetly filed,
must try where sword and tricky dagger failed.
—O rage of ripened hearts at grips with love!

Our heroes, wickedly entwined, have rolled
into the lynx-infested gulley where
their flesh will fertilize the greedy thorns;

the place is Hell, and crowded with our friends,
so leap right in, my heartless Amazon,
to keep our hatred's fire perpetual.

38 ❋ THE BALCONY

Mother of memories, absolute mistress,
in you my pleasure is my only task:
not to forget the form of a caress,
the dying fire and the alluring dark—
        mother of memories, absolute mistress!

Evenings illustrated by living coals
and evenings on the balcony, pink mist
rising, your soft breast, your gentle heart,
while we rehearsed the imperishable words—
        evenings illustrated by living coals.

How brilliant the sunsets, how warm the air,
how huge the sky: the size of our own souls.

Holding you, most loved—no, revered!
I could almost smell the fragrance of your blood—
    how brilliant the sunsets, how warm the air!

The night solidified into a wall,
and my eyes had to guess where yours would be
as I drank in your breath: nectar! venom!
and your feet lay still in my harmless hands:
    the night solidified into a wall.

I know the art of conjuring up delight,
and I relive my past buried in your lap;
for beauty languorous as yours recurs
only in your loved body, your loving heart:
    I know the art of conjuring up delight.

Those endless kisses, promises, perfumes:
is it forbidden to have them back again
out of the dark, like the sun rising new
out of its purgation in the sea?
    O endless kisses, promises, perfumes!

39 ✮ **POSSESSED**

The sun is in mourning. Be like the sun,
moon of my life, swathe yourself in crepe,
sleep, smoke, whatever—be still or glum,
plummet to the depths of boredom's pit—

I love you there. But if now your whim—
like the moon leaving her eclipse behind—
is to strut in the places where Folly throngs,
so be it! Lovely dagger, leave your sheath!

Light your eyes in the gas lamps' glow,
light others' with their lust for you...
Anything goes: sullen or submissive,

be what you will, black night, red dawn—
each nerve of my trembling body cries:
"Dear Demon, with this I thee worship!"

40 ❀ A PHANTOM

I
THE SHADOWS

Dejection has its catacombs
to which Fate has abandoned me;
no light comes, and I am left
with Night, a sullen cell-mate—

as if a scoffing God had forced
my hand to fresco...silhouettes!
Here with grisly appetite
I grill and devour my heart,

but then a shape looms, shining,
and as it moves it modifies:
a lovely...something—is there not

all the East in its easy way?
I know my visitor! *She* comes,
black—yet how that blackness glows!

II
THE PERFUME

Reader, you know how a church can reek
from one grain of incense you inhale
with careful greed—remember the smell?
Or the stubborn musk of an old sachet?

The spell is cast, the magic works,
and the present is the past—restored!
So a lover from beloved flesh
plucks subtle flowers of memory...

In bed her heavy resilient hair
—a living censer, like a sachet—
released its animal perfume,

and from discarded underclothes
still fervent with her sacred body's
form, there rose a scent of fur.

III
THE FRAME

As the fine frame completes a canvas
(even one from a master's hand),
adding an indefinable magic
by dividing art from mere nature,

so jewels, mirrors, metals, gold
invariably suited her loveliness—
none violated the luster she had,
and each thing seemed to set her off.

You might have said, sometimes, she thought
objects longed to make love to her,
so greedily she slaked her nakedness

on the kisses of linen sheets and silk,
revealing with each movement all
the unstudied grace of a marmoset.

IV
THE PORTRAIT

Look what Death and Disease have made
of our old flame: a heap of ashes.

My god, how horrible! What's left
of eyes so soft yet so intense,

of kisses stronger than any drug,
of a mouth that used to drown my heart,
of all our glowing exaltation?
Precious little—barely a sketch

fading in a solitude like mine,
erased a little more each day
by disrespectful Time that wipes

out Life and Art; yet even Time
cannot force me to forget Her
who was my glory and my Joy!

41 ✻ "SUPPOSE MY NAME…"

Suppose my name were favored by the winds,
my voyage prospered, and the future read
all that I wrote, and marveled…Love, they're yours!
I give you poems to make your memory

echo the way archaic legends do,
so that by some incantatory spell,
haunting the reader like a psaltery,
you will be caught within my cadences;

who now, from Pit to Empyrean
scorned by all but me, have simply walked away
and left no trace but shadows as you pass,

staring in mute composure at a world
that stupidly reviles your unconcern,
my jet-eyed statue, angel with brazen brows!

42 ❈ SEMPER EADEM

"You're like some rock the sea is swallowing—
what is it that brings on these moods of yours?"
Nothing mysterious: the ordinary pain
of being alive. You wouldn't understand,

though it's as obvious as that smile of yours:
an open secret. Nothing ever grows,
once the heart is harvested... You ask
too many questions. No more talking now,

my prying ignoramus, no more words,
however sweet your voice. You call it Life,
but Death is what binds us, and by subtler bonds...

Come here. The only lie that comforts me
is the refuge of those lashes—let me sink
into the silent fiction of your eyes!

43 ❈ ALTOGETHER

The Devil it must have been
who came to my room this morning
        and, trying to catch me out,
insisted I answer his question:

"Among the miracles
her spell over you comprises—
        among the black or pink
objects composing her body—

        which is dearest?' My soul
responded thus to the Demon:
        "No single part is best,
for each in its way is a solace,

and if the Whole enthralls,
is any detail the seducer?
      She dazzles like the dawn
and like the darkness consoles me;

      too close the harmony
that governs her lovely body
      for reason to divide
one rapture from another;

      my senses all are fused
by subtle transformation—
      her breathing makes a song,
as her voice emits a fragrance!"

44 ❋ "WHAT WILL YOU SAY TONIGHT..."

What will you say tonight, forsaken soul,
how will you speak, my long-since-withered heart,
to her, the loveliest and most beloved
whose sudden grace has made you green again?

—Singing her praises will be all our pride,
so peerless is the mercy of her power!
Sacred the fragrance that enrobes her flesh,
and ours, beneath her glance, is clad in light.

Whether we are in darkness and alone
or in the street and one among the crowd,
her spirit dances like a torch held high,

saying: "By my beauty I command,
love only beauty for my sake—I am
the Guardian Angel, Madonna, and the Muse."

45 ❋ THE LIVING TORCH

after Poe's To Helen

They pass before me, those electric eyes
some abstruse Angel must have magnetized—
celestial twins, yet mine as well, they pass
and share with me their supernatural power;

protecting me from trespasses and snares,
they lead to Beauty, as the poet says:
"They are my ministers—yet I their slave,"
and all my being serves that living torch.

Enchanting eyes! you glisten with the light
of candles burning in broad day—the sun
challenges but does not change their flame;

they burn for Death, you for the New Life:
you sing my soul's awakening—bright stars,
"Venuses unextinguished by the sun."

46 ❋ AGAINST HER LEVITY

You tilt your head and smile—as if
        across the countryside
a breeze had rippled through the grass
        out of a brilliant sky.

The sullen stranger you brush past
        stops, turns and relishes
the radiant health that aureoles
        your shoulders and your arms.

In all that panoply of silks
        the colors you parade

awaken in our poets' minds
  a giddy *valse des fleurs*—

garish gowns that designate
    the motley of your mind:
infectious folly! all I loathe
    is one with all I love!

Often, when I would drag myself
    into some leafy park
and when the sun like a rebuke
    would lacerate my breast,

so deeply did the Spring's new green
    humiliate my heart
that I would punish in one rose
    all Nature's insolence...

I'll come like that to you some night
    when lovers ought to come,
creeping in silence till I reach
    the treasures of your flesh,

to castigate your body's joy,
    to bruise your envied breasts,
and in your unsuspecting side
    to gash a gaping wound

where in a final ecstasy
    between those lovelier
new lips, my sister, I'll inject
    my venom into you!

47 ❋   REVERSIBILITY

Blithe as you are, what could you know of shame,
grief, remorse—of midnight's vague alarms

45

that treat the heart like a much-crumpled page
to be discarded with the morning's trash?
Being so blithe, what do you know of shame?

Fond as you are, what could you know of hate,
the secretly clenched fists, the silent tears,
while every heartbeat drums *revenge! revenge!*
and one by one our talents are enslaved—
being so fond, what do you know of hate?

Hale as you are, what could you know of death
whose fevers worm their way like prisoners
past the high walls of the white infirmary,
seeking a patch of sun—what do they whisper?
Being so hale, what do you know of death?

Fair as you are, what could you know of fear—
the fear of ageing and the unspeakable pain
of finding only half-concealed disgust
in eyes from which we once drank greedily!
Being so fair, what do you know of fear?

Warm as you are, so radiant with life
a dying David would have begged for health
from the enchanting presence of your flesh—
but all I dare to beg for is your prayers,
warm as you are, so radiant with life!

48 ❋ CONFESSION

Once, indulgent lady—only once
        you lay your lustrous arm
on mine (against the darkness of my soul
        the incident stands out);

as if it had just been coined, a golden moon
        rose ostentatiously,

and night's magnificence, while Paris slept,
    streamed like another Seine.

Along the housefronts, out of every door
    appeared attentive cats,
following like companionable ghosts
    or frozen as we passed.

And even as our intimacy bloomed
    in that pale radiance,
there came from you—and from that instrument
    of yours, a voice so rich

habitually, exultant as a peal
    of trumpets in the dawn—
there came a sound, a sigh, a plaintive note
    that faltered on your lips

like a sickly, hideous, misproportioned child,
    the family disgrace
long secluded from the world's regard
    in some dark hideaway.

"Nothing!" it sobbed, that sudden note of yours,
    "nothing on earth is sure,
and all our human masks cannot disguise
    our human selfishness;

Beauty is merely woman's livelihood,
    a well-rehearsed routine—
the flagging dancer's discipline: to please
    with automatic smiles;

hearts are not to be depended on,
    they fail—like beauty and love,
until Oblivion gathers up the lot
    for good, all over again!"

That magic moon has never left my mind,
    that silence, that fatigue,
and that dead secret whispered in despair
    at the heart's confessional.

49 ✻   SPIRITUAL DAWN

Even licentious beds are touched by dawn
and its relentless Absolute—as if
the operation of some vengeful power
wakened an angel in the sleeping beast.

To fallen man, who suffers and dreams on,
the Empyrean's inaccessible blue
presents the fascination of the Void.
Beloved Goddess, so it is with you—

above the wreck of stupid revelry
your lucid image rises, brighter still,
shimmering yet fixed before my eyes.

The sun has turned the smoking torches black;
so it is with you, resplendent soul—
your phantom triumphs like the immortal sun!

50 ✻   EVENING HARMONY

Now comes the time when swaying on its stem
each flower offers incense to the night;
phrases and fragrances circle in the dark—
languorous waltz that casts a lingering spell!

Each flower offers incense to the night;
the violin trembles like a heart betrayed—
languorous waltz that casts a lingering spell!
A mournful altar ornaments the sky.

The violin trembles like a heart betrayed,
a tender heart unnerved by nothingness!
A mournful altar ornaments the sky;
the sun has smothered in its clotting blood.

A tender heart unnerved by nothingness
hoards every fragment of the radiant past.
The sun has smothered in its clotting blood.
In me your image—like a monstrance—glows.

51 ❋ THE FLASK

Some scents can permeate all substances—
even glass seems porous to their power.
Opening an Oriental chest
once the reluctant locks are pried apart,

or an armoire in some abandoned house
acrid with the dust of time itself,
may yield a musty flask that keeps the faith:
out of it leaps a returning soul—alive!

Like chrysalides, a thousand memories
that slept among the silent shadows now
unfold their wings and soar into the light,
rising azure laced with rose and gold;

among them one intoxicating thought
hovers brightest; eyes close; Vertigo
grips the beaten soul that it impels
to an abyss obscured by human wraiths,

crushing it on the brink of that age-old pit
where, like a fetid Lazarus rending his shroud,
the corpse of an old passion stirs and wakes,
spectral and rancid, charnel and charming still!

So it will be with me when I lie lost
to living memory, a used-up flask
tossed in a grim armoire, tarnished and cracked,
forgotten, filthy, a decrepit thing:

I shall be your coffin, darling doom,
and testify to how your virulence—
the poison angels brewed—became in me
the consummation of a heart consumed!

52 ✵ POISON

Wine can endow the lowest dive
        with sudden luxury
and out of a red mist create
        enchanted porticoes,
like sunset firing a sodden sky.

Opium can dilate boundless space
        and plumb eternity,
emptying out time itself
        till a grim ecstasy
burdens the soul past all bearing.

—None of which equals the poison
        welling up in your eyes
that show me my poor soul reversed...
        My dreams throng to drink
at those green, distorting pools.

—None of which rivals the taste
        of your bitter saliva
that like a pestilence infects
        my soul until it sinks
unconscious on the shores of death!

53 ❋ OVERCAST

Are they blue, gray, or green? Mysterious eyes
(as if in fact you were looking through a mist)
in alternation tender, dreamy, grim
to match the shiftless pallor of the sky.

That's what you're like—these warm white afternoons
that make the ravished heart dissolve in tears,
the nerves, inexplicably overwrought,
outrage the dozing mind. Not always, though—

sometimes you're like the horizon when the sun
ignites our cloudy autumn—how you glow!
a sodden countryside in sudden rout,
turned incandescent by a changing wind.

Dangerous woman—demoralizing days!
Will I adore your killing frost as much,
and in that implacable winter, when it comes,
discover pleasures sharper than iron and ice?

54 ❋ CAT

As if he owned the place, a cat
    meanders through my mind,
sleek and proud, yet so discreet
    in making known his will

that I hear music when he mews,
    and even when he purrs
a tender timbre in the sound
    compels my consciousness—

a secret rhythm penetrates
    to unsuspected depths,

obsessive as a line of verse
    and potent as a drug:

all woes are spirited away,
    I hear ecstatic news—
it seems a telling language has
    no need of words at all.

My heart, assenting instrument,
    is masterfully played;
no other bow across its strings
    can draw such music out

the way this cat's uncanny voice
    —seraphic, alien—
can reconcile discordant strains
    into close harmony!

One night his brindled fur gave off
    a perfume so intense
I seemed to be embalmed because
    (just once!) I fondled him...

Familiar spirit, genius, judge,
    the cat presides—inspires
events that he appears to spurn,
    half goblin and half god!

and when my spellbound eyes at last
    relinquish worship of
this cat they love to contemplate
    and look inside myself,

I find to my astonishment
    like living opals there
his fiery pupils, embers that
    observe me fixedly.

55 ❋ THE FINE SHIP

I want to tell you, soft enchantress, all
the various graces that array your youth;
     I want to paint your beauty for you
in which the woman merges with the girl.

Walk, and your wide skirts swirl with every step,
as if a fine ship had put out to sea
     under full sail, riding the waves
to a gentle rhythm, indolent and slow.

Above plump shoulders and a pliant throat
your head parades, a preening miracle!
     With a look of placid mastery
you pass upon your way, majestic child.

I want to tell you, soft enchantress, all
the various graces that array your youth;
     I want to paint your beauty for you
in which the woman merges with the girl.

The swelling silk that cradles your full breasts
makes them—triumphant breasts!—a sleek armoire
     whose bright and curving surfaces
reflect the light as if from flashing shields,

provocative shields, armed with rosy points!
Armoire of secrets, crammed with precious things—
     perfumes and wines and rare liqueurs
to make our hearts and minds delirious!

Walk, and your wide skirts swirl with every step,
as if a fine ship had put out to sea
     under full sail, riding the waves
to a gentle rhythm, indolent and slow.

Your noble thighs, beneath the tossing lace,
arouse obscure desires and vex them like
      two witches who between them stir
a black elixir in their seething vat.

Your arms would serve an infant Hercules
against the gleaming serpents they are like,
      relentless in their coiled embrace—
as though to print your lover on your heart.

Above plump shoulders and a pliant throat
your head parades, a preening miracle!
      With a look of placid mastery
you pass upon your way, majestic child.

56 ❋   INVITATION TO THE VOYAGE

      Imagine the magic
      of living together
there, with all the time in the world
      for loving each other,
      for loving and dying
where even the landscape resembles you:
      the suns dissolved
      in overcast skies
have the same mysterious charm for me
      as your wayward eyes
      through crystal tears,
         my sister, my child!

All is order there, and elegance,
      pleasure, peace, and opulence.

      Furniture gleaming
      with the patina
of time itself in the room we would share;
      the rarest flowers

mingling aromas
with amber's uncertain redolence;
encrusted ceilings
echoed in mirrors
and Eastern splendor on the walls—
here all would whisper
to the soul in secret
her sweet mother tongue.

All is order there, and elegance,
pleasure, peace, and opulence.

On these still canals
the freighters doze
fitfully: their mood is for roving,
and only to flatter
a lover's fancy
have they put in from the ends of the earth.
By late afternoon
the canals catch fire
as sunset glorifies the town;
the world turns to gold
as it falls asleep
in a fervent light.

All is order there, and elegance,
pleasure, peace, and opulence.

57 ❋ THE IRREPARABLE

Who can destroy this old, this long Remorse
that fastens on our heart
and fattens there like weevils in an oak
or vermin on a corpse?
How shall we kill implacable Remorse?

What drug, what wine is warranted to drown
        this ancient enemy
greedier and more wanton than the whores,
        more patient than the ants?
Who will brew that potion, draw that wine?

If you know the secret, tell it, lovely witch,
        to one who waits in dread,
abandoned like a wounded soldier crushed
        by panic-stricken hooves.
Tell all you know, beloved sorceress,

to a dying man the wolves already sniff
        and carrion-crows await,
to a fallen warrior! Must he despair
        of a cross to mark his grave,
fallen a victim to such predators?

What wind can sweep the ashes from this sky,
        what stars can pierce the gloom
that never deepens, never pales—a night
        no lightning ever rends?
Ashes fill this sky, and darkness reigns.

Hope's candle at a window of the inn
        glimmers and goes out.
No light, no moon—how will they find their way,
        the martyrs of the road?
Satan has snuffed the candle at the inn!

Adorable siren, do you love the damned?
        What do you know of Remorse
whose poisoned arrows mercilessly take
        our heart for their target?
Adorable siren, do you love the damned?

Nothing can withstand the Irreparable—
        its termites undermine

our soul, pathetic citadel, until
    the ruined tower falls.
Nothing can withstand the Irreparable!

—More than once, in a wretched theater
    ringing with cheap tunes,
I've seen a goddess change the livid sky
    to a miraculous dawn;
there have been times, in such a theater,

when I've beheld a creature made of light
    defeat Satan himself;
but only there. On my heart's stage occurs
    no transformation scene.
No creature made of light will come to me!

58 ❋ CONVERSATION (ONE SIDE)

Fresh as an autumn morning you may be,
yet sadness rises in me like the sea
that ebbing leaves a bitter after-taste
of iodine on my still-smarting lips.

No use your groping for my feeble heart—
what you are after is no longer there;
mauled by women's weapons, fangs and claws,
my heart is gone, the beasts have eaten it.

My heart! that palace ransacked by a mob
of drunken maenads at each other's throats...
What perfume hovers round *your* naked throat?

O Beauty, scourge of souls, thy will be done!
With eyes as bright as candles at a feast,
consume these scraps of flesh the beasts have spared!

59 ✻ AUTUMNAL

1

Soon cold shadows will close over us
and summer's transitory gold be gone;
I hear them chopping firewood in our court—
the dreary thud of logs on cobblestone.

Winter will come to repossess my soul
with rage and outrage, horror, drudgery,
and like the sun in its polar holocaust
my heart will be a block of blood-red ice.

I listen trembling to that grim tattoo—
build a gallows, it would sound the same.
My mind becomes a tower giving way
under the impact of a battering-ram.

Stunned by the strokes, I seem to hear, somewhere,
a coffin hurriedly hammered shut—for whom?
Summer was yesterday; autumn is here!
Strange how that sound rings out like a farewell.

2

How sweet the greenish light of your long eyes!
But even that turns bitter now, and nothing
—not love, the boudoir, nor its busy hearth—
can match the summer's radiance on the sea.

Love me still, my darling! mother me,
ungrateful though I am, your naughty boy.
Sister and mistress! be the fleeting warmth
of a sumptuous autumn or a setting sun.

Your chore will be brief—the grave is covetous!
so let me rest my forehead on your knees

and relish, as I mourn white summer's lapse,
the yellow favor of the waning year.

60 ❋ **To a Madonna**

EX-VOTO IN THE SPANISH TASTE

Madonna, my mistress, I shall build for you
an altar hidden in the heart of my despair
and in my heart itself, the darkest part—
far from worldly zeal and worldly scorn—
shall carve a niche enameled blue and gold
to shield the awesome Image shining there.
Out of my Verses wrought to golden threads
on which the crystal rhymes are strung like beads
I'll plait a crown to set upon your head,
and from my Jealousy, O mortal queen,
I'll weave a Mantle in barbaric style—
embroidered not with pearls but with my Tears!—
stiff with Suspicion that will line the whole,
imprisoning your charms as in a Tower.
As for your Dress—it will be my Desire,
shimmering and rippling round your flesh,
rising to those headlands where it hovers,
warming your body's porcelain with a kiss.
Ingeniously sewn, my Reverence
will make you satin Slippers that assume
in all humility the shape your feet
impose upon their soft imprisonment;
and if I fail, despite my diligence,
to forge a silver Footstool from the Moon,
I'll set the Serpent that my entrails feed
under your Heel, triumphant queen from whom
Redemption flows, to signify you flout
this monster varicose with hate and spleen.
Behold my Thoughts arrayed like votive lights
among the flowers on my Lady's shrine,
spangling the azure ceiling as they gaze

on you eternally with eyes of fire!
And since my every impulse worships you,
all will become as Myrrh and Frankincense
mounting in troubled vapors from my Soul
to reach the snowy region where you stand.

Lastly, to assure you Mary's role,
by mixing love with cruelty I'll turn
the Seven Deadly Sins into keen swords
as a remorseful executioner
relishing nonetheless his dismal charge,
and with a juggler's unconcern I'll make
a target of your inexhaustible Love
and plunge them all within your sobbing Heart—
within your throbbing Heart, your bleeding Heart!

61 ❀   SONG FOR LATE IN THE DAY

Although your wicked brows belie
     the angel in your eyes,
it is a blessed sorcery
     by which I am beguiled:

with all the ineffectual awe
     of prostrate votaries
I worship at your trivial
     and tantalizing shrine!

Wilderness and desert haunt
     the tumult of your hair;
without a word, your lips propose
     the riddle of the Sphinx;

and when you move, the shifting scent—
     as if a censer swayed—
prepares the advent of your flesh:
     the night is warm with you.

Where is the drug that works as well
      as your untroubled sloth?
You know the secret: at your touch
      the dead return to life;

there is a throbbing intercourse
      between your breasts and thighs—
the very cushions are enticed
      by your slow attitudes.

Occasionally, to assuage
      mysterious appetites,
your lazy kisses alternate
      with unexpected bites,

and as you laugh you lacerate
      my undefended skin,
then gentle as the rising moon
      you raise your eyes to mine...

Beneath your satin slippers, as
      beneath your silken feet,
I lay my hopes of happiness,
      my genius, and my fate—

light of my life, my soul's release,
      I long for your embrace:
explode in one dissolving blast
      this black Siberia!

62 ✶ SISINA

Imagine Diana, followed by her troupe,
beating the bushes in hot pursuit of game,
hair flying, breast bare, reveling in the din,
proudly outdistancing the pride of the hunt!

And have you seen our "Fury of the Gironde,"
grimly urging on a barefoot mob,
cheeks and eyes radiant as she climbs
the palace stairs, a saber in her fist?

Sisina's like that! Except the wild girl
has a soul as loving as it is incensed,
and her courage, roused by cannon fire and drums,

will yet relent to passionate appeal,
and her incandescent heart still keeps,
for the deserving, a reservoir of tears.

63 ❀ ## To a Creole Lady

The isle is fragrant and the sun is kind;
shadows of palm and poinciana shed
their languor on a lady living there
unknown to men's acclaim. I know her, though:

warm and white beneath a cloud of hair,
her face is borne with noble elegance—
she walks like Artemis, as tall, as lithe,
and when she smiles, assurance lights her glance…

If you should ever visit glory's home
along the green Loire or the Seine, Madame,
your loveliness, a match for our chateaux,

would prompt in "scholarly retreats" a flood
of sonnets from our poets' hearts, enslaved
more humbly than your blacks by those great eyes.

64 ✸ MOESTA ET ERRABUNDA

Lady, do you sometimes long to escape
from the filth of the city, from this black sea
to one whose everlasting splendor glows
blue, bright and deep—a virgin sea!
Lady, do you sometimes long to escape?

The titan sea console us for our toil!
What demon gave that raucous amateur
supported by the organ of the winds
the sacred task of singing lullabies?
The titan sea console us for our toil?

By wheel or sail, just take me anywhere
far from here where mud is made of our tears!
Lady, listen to your heart; doesn't it say
"Far from regret, from crime, from suffering,
by wheel or sail, just take me anywhere"?

How far away, that fragrant paradise
where love and pleasure share the same blue sky,
where pure delight can satiate the heart
and all we love is worthy of our love!
How far away, that fragrant paradise!

But that green paradise of puppy love,
of songs and games, of kisses and bouquets—
the jugs of wine at evening in the groves,
the violins that die behind the hills—
but that green paradise of puppy love,

the innocent paradise of timid joys,
is it already farther than Cathay?
What silvery voice can waken it again,
what plaintive cries can ever call it back,
the innocent paradise of timid joys?

65 ❋ INCUBUS

Eyes glowing like an angel's
I'll come back to your bed
and reach for you from the shadows:
you won't hear a thing.

On your dark skin my kisses
will be colder than moonlight:
caresses of a snake crawling
round an open grave.

When the morning whitens
you find no one beside you:
the place cold all day.

Others by fondness prevail
over your life, your youth:
I leave it to fear.

66 ❋ AUTUMN SONNET

I read the question in your crystal eyes:
"Why do you love me, my strange lover?" Stay
lovely and keep still! Outraged by all
except the innocence of beasts, my heart

will not reveal its secret pact with Hell,
the livid legend written out in flames,
to you whose arms would cradle me in sleep.
Passion offends me, and my mind is pain!

Hold me. Say nothing. Hidden somewhere near,
Love in ambush bends his fatal bow—
I know the weapons of that old armory:

madness, horror, crime...You pale and stare
like an autumn daisy, flower of the fall,
white as your wintry Faust, cold Marguerite.

67 ✻ SORROWS OF THE MOON

Tonight the moon dreams still more languidly:
as if some beauty on her pillowed couch
were brushing with a half-unconscious hand
the contour of her breasts before she fell

asleep. On a silken avalanche of clouds
the moon, expiring, falls into a trance,
impassive as the great white visions file
past in procession like unfolding flowers.

And when she happens, in her somnolence,
to shed a secret tear that falls to earth,
some eager poet, sleep's sworn enemy,

cups his hand and catches that pale tear
that shimmers like a shard of opal there,
and hides it from the sun's eye in his heart.

68 ✻ CATS

Lovers, scholars—the fervent, the austere—
grow equally fond of cats, their household pride.
As sensitive as either to the cold,
as sedentary, though so strong and sleek,

your cat, a friend to learning and to love,
seeks out both silence and the awesome dark...
Hell would have made the cat its courier
could it have controverted feline pride!

Dozing, all cats assume the svelte design
of desert sphinxes sprawled in solitude,
apparently transfixed by endless dreams;

their teeming loins are rich in magic sparks,
and golden specks like infinitesimal sand
glisten in those enigmatic eyes.

69 ✻ OWLS

Under black yews that protect them
    the owls perch in a row
like alien gods whose red eyes
    glitter. They meditate.

Petrified, they will perch there till
    the melancholy hour
when the slanting sun is ousted,
    and darkness settles down.

    From their posture, the wise
learn to shun, in this world at least,
    motion and commotion;

impassioned by passing shadows,
    man will always be scourged
for trying to change his place.

70 ✻ THE PIPE

I am a writer's pipe. One look at me,
and the coffee color of my Kaffir face
will tell you I am not the only slave:
my master is addicted to his vice.

Every so often he is overcome
by some despair or other, whereupon
tobacco clouds pour out of me as if
the stove were kindled and the pot put on.

I wrap his soul in mine and cradle it
within a blue and fluctuating thread
that rises out of my rekindled lips

from the glowing coal that brews a secret spell.
He smokes his pipe, allaying heart and mind,
and for tonight all injuries are healed.

71 ✱ **MUSIC**

BEETHOVEN

Music often takes me like a sea
            and I set out
under mist or a transparent sky
            for my pale star;

I run before the wind as if I had
            laid on full sail,
climbing the mountainous backs of the waves,
            plummeting down

in darkness, eardrums throbbing as I feel
            the coming wreck;
fair winds or foul—a raging storm

            on the great deep
my cradle, and dead calm the looking-glass
            of my despair!

72 ❀ Burial

Surely *some* night will be dark enough
  for a kindly Christian soul
to dump your gorgeous body, now deceased,
  where the other garbage goes;

decent planets, at a time like this,
  renounce their vigilance—
the spider has her web to tidy up,
  the viper's brood must hatch;

and over your unconsecrated head
  you'll hear the howling wolves
lament their fate and yours the livelong year;

the coven gathers—famished hags excite
  old men to do their worst,
while killers dice for victims on your grave.

73 ❀ A Fantastic Engraving

Uncanny apparition—all it wears,
grotesquely canted on that grinning skull,
is a garland woven out of worms! No spurs.
no whip, and still this ghostly cavalier
urges his apocalyptic nag
onward till her flaring nostrils bleed,
horse and horseman mad in pursuit of Space,
trampling Infinity with reckless hooves!
The rider brandishes a flaming sword
above the nameless hordes he gallops down,
and like a prince inspecting his domain
quarters that unending graveyard where
a bleak white sun exposes, mile on mile,
history's hecatombs, ancient and modern both.

74 ❋ THE HAPPY CORPSE

Wherever the soil is rich and full of snails
I want to dig myself a nice deep grave—
deep enough to stretch out these old bones
and sleep in peace, like a shark in the cradling wave.

Testaments and tombstones always lie!
Before collecting such official grief,
I'd rather ask the crows, while I'm alive,
to pick my carcass clean from end to end.

They may be deaf and blind, my friends the worms,
yet surely they will welcome a happy corpse;
feasting philosophers, scions of decay,

eat your way through me without a second thought
and let me know if one last twinge is left
for a soulless body deader than the dead!

75 ❋ THE CASK OF HATE

Hate is the Cask of the Danaïdes;
even Vengeance, frenzied and red-armed,
cannot replenish those depths fast enough
with bucketfuls of blood and dead men's tears—

Hell thirsts on, mysterious holes appear
and through them seep a thousand years of toil,
despite the victims desperately slain
and brought to life to suffer once again.

Or Hate is a drunk at the dark end of the bar
whose liquor only makes him thirstier—
a Hydra multiplies in every drop;

happy the man who drinks to meet his fate,
but Hate is fettered to a fiercer doom
and cannot even drink himself to death.

76 ✸ THE CRACKED BELL

Bitter, but sweet as well! on winter nights
when embers whiten on the hearth, to hear
faraway memories slowly surfacing,
summoned by carillons chiming through the mist.

Blessèd be the rugged-throated bell,
alert and tough for all its years, that tolls
religiously the watches of the night
like some old trooper standing sentinel!

My soul is cracked, and when in its distress
it tries to sing the chilly nights away,
how often its enfeebled voice suggests

the gasping of a wounded soldier left
beside a lake of blood, who, pinned beneath
a pile of dead men, struggles, stares and dies.

77 ✸ SPLEEN (I)

February, peeved at Paris, pours
a gloomy torrent on the pale lessees
of the graveyard next door and a mortal chill
on tenants of the foggy suburbs too.

The tiles afford no comfort to my cat
that cannot keep its mangy body still;
the soul of some old poet haunts the drains
and howls as if a ghost could hate the cold.

A church bell grieves, a log in the fireplace smokes
and hums falsetto to the clock's catarrh,
while in a filthy reeking deck of cards

inherited from a dropsical old maid,
the dapper Knave of Hearts and the Queen of Spades
grimly disinter their love affairs.

78 ❀ SPLEEN (II)

Souvenirs?
More than if I had lived a thousand years!

No chest of drawers crammed with documents,
love letters, wedding invitations, wills,
a lock of someone's hair rolled up in a deed,
hides so many secrets as my brain.
This branching catacomb, this pyramid
contains more corpses than the potter's field:
I am a graveyard that the moon abhors,
where long worms like regrets come out to feed
most ravenously on my dearest dead.
I am an old boudoir where a rack of gowns,
perfumed by withered roses, rots to dust;
where only faint pastels and pale Bouchers
inhale the scent of long-unstoppered flasks.

Nothing is slower than the limping days
when under the heavy weather of the years
Boredom, the fruit of glum indifference,
gains the dimension of eternity...
Hereafter, mortal clay, you are no more
than a rock encircled by a nameless dread,
an ancient sphinx omitted from the map,
forgotten by the world, and whose fierce moods
sing only to the rays of setting suns.

79 ❋ SPLEEN (III)

I'm like the king of a rainy country, rich
but helpless, decrepit though still a young man
who scorns his fawning tutors, wastes his time
on dogs and other animals, and has no fun;
nothing distracts him, neither hawk nor hound
nor subjects starving at the palace gate.
His favorite fool's obscenities fall flat
—the royal invalid is not amused—
and ladies in waiting for a princely nod
no longer dress indecently enough
to win a smile from this young skeleton.
The bed of state becomes a stately tomb.
The alchemist who brews him gold has failed
to purge the impure substance from his soul,
and baths of blood, Rome's legacy recalled
by certain barons in their failing days,
are useless to revive this sickly flesh
through which no blood but brackish Lethe seeps.

80 ❋ SPLEEN (IV)

When skies are low and heavy as a lid
over the mind tormented by disgust,
and hidden in the gloom the sun pours down
on us a daylight dingier than the dark;

when earth becomes a trickling dungeon where
Trust like a bat keeps lunging through the air,
beating tentative wings along the walls
and bumping its head against the rotten beams;

when rain falls straight from unrelenting clouds,
forging the bars of some enormous jail,

and silent hordes of obscene spiders spin
their webs across the basements of our brains;

then all at once the raging bells break loose,
hurling to heaven their awful caterwaul,
like homeless ghosts with no one left to haunt
whimpering their endless grievances.

—And giant hearses, without dirge or drums,
parade at half-step in my soul, where Hope,
defeated, weeps, and the oppressor Dread
plants his black flag on my assenting skull.

81 ✿ **OBSESSION**

Forest, I fear you! in my ruined heart
your roaring wakens the same agony
as in cathedrals when the organ moans
and from the depths I hear that I am damned.

Ocean, I hate you! for I recognize
the sobs and insults of my own despair,
the bitter laughter of a beaten man
repeated in the sea's huge gaiety.

Night! you'd please me more without these stars
that speak a language I know all too well—
I long for darkness, silence, *nothing there...*

Yet even shadows have their shapes that live
where I imagine them to be, the hordes
of vanished souls whose eyes acknowledge mine.

82 ❀ CRAVING FOR OBLIVION

Once you were hot for battle, weary mind!
Now Hope, whose spur awakened all your zeal,
no longer even mounts. No shame in that—
lie down, old horse! You stumble at each step.

Abandon Hope, and sleep the sleep of the beasts.

Defeated mind, old plunderer! For you
love has no more seduction than your sword.
Farewell to lutes and trumpet calls alike—
such pleasures cannot tempt a sullen heart,

and even Spring has lost its sweet allure.

Moment by moment, Time envelops me
like a stiffening body buried in the snow...
I contemplate the infinitesimal globe,
and I no longer seek asylum there.

Avalanche, entomb me in your fall!

83 ❀ ALCHEMY OF SUFFERING

Nature glows with this man's joy,
        dims with another's grief;
what signifies the grave to one
        is glory to the next.

Trismegistus intercedes:
        this ever-daunting guide
makes me a Midas in reverse,
        saddest of alchemists—

gold turns iron at my touch,
    heaven darkens to hell;
clouds become a winding-sheet

    to shroud my cherished dead,
and on celestial shores I build
    enormous sepulchres.

84 ❋ SYMPATHETIC HORROR

When the sky appears in pain
and sunset no more than a wound,
what are the thoughts that occur
to a libertine soul like yours?

—Nothing can slake my thirst
for the nameless and the obscure:
you'll never hear me complain
like Ovid whining for Rome.

The canyons of bloody cloud
accommodate my pride,
their nebulous shapes become

a splendid hearse for my dreams,
their red glow the reflection
of the Hell where my heart's at home.

85 ❋ HEAUTON TIMOROUMENOS*

No rage, no rancor: I shall beat you
    as butchers fell an ox,
as Moses smote the rock in Horeb—
    I shall make you weep,

*Self-Tormentor, title of a play by Terence. Baudelaire took his last line from Poe's "Haunted Palace."

75

and by the waters of affliction
       my desert will be slaked.
My desire, that hope has made monstrous,
       will frolic in your tears

as a ship tosses on the ocean—
       in my besotted heart
your adorable sobs will echo
       like an ecstatic drum.

For I—am I not a dissonance
       in the divine accord,
because of the greedy Irony
       that infiltrates my soul?

I hear it in my voice—that shrillness,
       that poison in my blood!
I am the sinister glass in which
       the Fury sees herself!

I am the knife and the wound it deals,
       I am the slap and the cheek,
I am the wheel and the broken limbs,
       hangman and victim both!

I am the vampire at my own veins,
       one of the great lost horde
doomed for the rest of time, and beyond,
       "to laugh—but smile no more."

86 ❋ THE IRREMEDIABLE

I

A Form, an Idea, a Being
       out of the Blue—and fallen

into a Stygian morass
      far from the eye of heaven...

Lured by the love of chaos,
      an Angel, unwary pilgrim

caught in Nightmare's current,
      struggling like a swimmer

pitted in deadly panic
      against the howling vortex,
whirling and faster whirled
      down, down and under

Groping for key or candle,
      a wretch in some witch's thrall
rots in her snaky den
      with no hope of escaping...

A soul in torment descending
      endless rickety stairs
into an echoing cavern
      out of which rises the stench

of vigilant slimy monsters
      whose luminous eyes enforce
the gloom, disclosing nothing
      except their own existence...

A schooner caught in the ice floes
      as in a crystal quicksand,
pursuing the fatal channel
      that led to this prison...

Apt emblems, properties
      of irremediable Fate,
proving how consummately
      Satan consumes his own!

2

Distinct the heart's exchange
    with its own dark mirror,
for deep in that Well of Truth
    trembles one pale star,

ironic, infernal beacon,
    graceful torch of the Devil,
our solace and sole glory—
    consciousness in Evil!

87 ✸ THE CLOCK

Impassive god! whose minatory hands
repeat their sinister and single charge:
Remember! Pain is the unfailing bow,
as arrow after arrow finds your heart.

Pleasure fades and dances out of sight—
one pirouette, the theater goes dark;
each instant snatches from you what you had,
the crumb of happiness within your grasp.

Thirty-six hundred times in every hour
the Second whispers: *Remember!* and Now replies
in its maddening mosquito hum: I am Past,
who passing lit and sucked your life and left!

Remember! Souviens-toi! Esto memor!
(My metal throat is polyglot.) The ore
of mortal minutes crumbles, unrefined,
from which your golden nuggets must be panned.

Remember! Time, that tireless gambler, wins
on every turn of the wheel: that is the law.

78

The daylight fades...*Remember*! Night comes on:
the pit is thirsty and the sands run out...

Soon it will sound, the tocsin of your Fate—
from noble Virtue, your still-virgin bride,
or from Repentance, last resort...from all
the message comes: "Too late, old coward! Die!

PARISIAN SCENES

88 ❋ Parisian Landscape

To make my eclogues proper, I must sleep
hard by heaven—like the astrologers—
and being the belfries' neighbor, hear in my dreams
their solemn anthems fading on the wind.
My garret view, perused attentively,
reveals the workshops and their singing slaves,
the city's masts—steeples and chimneypots—
and above that fleet, a blue eternity...

How sweet to see the first star in the sky,
the first lamp at the window through the mist,
the coalsmoke streaming upward, and the moon
shedding a pale enchantment on it all!
From there I'll watch the easy seasons pass
and when the tedious winter snows me in,
I'll close my shutters, draw the curtains snug,
and build my Spanish castles in the dark,
dreaming of alluring distances,
of sobbing fountains and of birds that sing
endless obbligatos to my trysts—
of everything in Idylls that's inane!
A revolution down in the street will not
distract me from my desk, for I shall be
committed to that almost carnal joy
of fastening the springtime to my will,
drawing the sun from my heart, and by my zeal
persuading Paris to become a South.

89 ❋ The Sun

Late in this cruel season when the sun
scourges alike the city and the fields,
parching the stubble and sinking into slums
where shuttered hovels hide vile appetites,

I venture out alone to drill myself
in what must seem an eerie fencing match,
dueling in dark corners for a rhyme
and stumbling over words like cobblestones
where now and then realities collide
with lines I dreamed of writing long ago.

What greensickness could stand up to the sun,
that towering foster father who dissolves
anxieties into air like morning mist,
ripening here a verse and there a rose
with honey on the tongue as in the hive?
Who but the sun persuades the lame to dance
as if their canes were maypoles, governing
the resurrection of the harrowed fields,
and for the secret harvest of the heart
commands immortal wheat to grow again!

When, with a poet's will, the sun descends
into the cities like a king incognito,
impartially visiting palace and hospital,
the fate of all things vile is glorified.

90 ❋ TO A RED-HAIRED BEGGAR GIRL

Gaping tatters in each garment prove
your calling is not only beggary
    but beauty as well,

and to a poet equally "reduced,"
the frail and freckled body you display
    makes its own appeal—

queens in velvet buskins take the stage
less regally than you wade through the mud
    on your wooden clogs.

What if, instead of these indecent rags,
the splendid train of a brocaded gown
    rustled at your heels,

and rather than torn stockings, just suppose
curious glances sliding up your thigh
    met with a gold dirk!

And then if, for our sins, those flimsy knots
released two perfect little breasts that shine
    brighter than your eyes,

and your own arms consented to reveal
the rest, though archly feigning to fend off
    hands that go too far…

Strands of pearls and strophes by Belleau
arriving in—imagine!—endless streams
    "from an admirer";

riffraff—talented and otherwise—
offering tributes to the slippered feet
    glimpsed from below stairs;

gentlemen sending flunkeys to find out
who owns the carriage always told to "wait"
    at your smart address

where, in the boudoir, kisses count for more
than quarterings, although the cast includes
    a Bourbon or two!

—Meanwhile, here you are, begging scraps
doled out by the local *table d'hôte*
    at the kitchen door

and scavenging discarded finery
worth forty sous, a price that (pardon me!)
I cannot afford...

Go, then, my Beauty, with no ornament
—patchouli or pearl choker—but your own
starveling nakedness!

91 ❋ THE SWAN

to Victor Hugo

I

Andromache, I think of you! That stream,
the sometime witness to your widowhood's
enormous majesty of mourning—that
mimic Simoïs salted by your tears

suddenly inundates my memory
as I cross the new Place du Carrousel.
Old Paris is gone (no human heart
changes half so fast as a city's face)

and only in my mind's eye can I see
the junk laid out to glitter in the booths
among the weeds and splintered capitals,
blocks of marble blackened by the mud;

there used to be a poultry market here,
and one cold morning—with the sky swept clean,
the ground, too, swept by garbagemen who raised
clouds of soot in the icy air—I saw

a swan that had broken out of its cage,
webbed feet clumsy on the cobblestones,

white feathers dragging in the uneven ruts,
and obstinately pecking at the drains,

drenching its enormous wings in the filth
as if in its own lovely lake, crying
"Where is the thunder, when will it rain?"
I see it still, inevitable myth,

like Daedalus dead-set against the sky—
the sky quite blue and blank and unconcerned—
that straining neck and that voracious beak,
as if the swan were castigating God!

2

Paris changes...But in sadness like mine
nothing stirs—new buildings, old
neighborhoods turn to allegory,
and memories weigh more than stone.

One image, near the Louvre, will not dissolve:
I think of that great swan in its torment,
silly, like all exiles, and sublime,
endlessly longing...And again I think

of you, Andromache, dragged off
to be the booty of Achilles' son,
Hector's widow now the wife of Helenus,
crouching blindly over an empty grave!

I think of some black woman, starving
and consumptive in the muddy streets,
peering through a wall of fog for those
missing palms of splendid Africa;

I think of orphans withering like flowers;
of those who lose what never can be found

again—never! swallowing their tears
and nursing at the she-wolf Sorrow's dugs;

and in the forest of my mind's exile
a merciless memory winds its horn:
I hear it and I think of prisoners,
of the shipwrecked, the beaten—and so many more!

92 ❋ THE SEVEN OLD MEN

to Victor Hugo

Swarming city—city gorged with dreams,
where ghosts by day accost the passer-by,
where secrets run in these defiled canals
like blood that gushes through a giant's veins!

One morning when the rain in these mean streets
made houses grimmer than the docks that line
the two banks of a filthy river, and
a yellow fog engulfed the space between—

a stage-effect to match the actor's mood—
I roamed as if in search of stern resolve
and arguments to steel my flagging soul
through backstreets shaken by each heavy van.

And out of nowhere came a wretch in rags
the very color of the dripping sky—
surely *this* deserved some charity!
But then I saw the malice in his eyes

and seemed to feel the cold because of them—
as if their pupils had been soaked in bile.
His beard stuck out as stiff as any sword
(Judas must have had a beard like that).

He wasn't bent, he was *broken*, and his spine
formed so sharp an angle with his legs
that his stick, as if to add a finishing touch,
gave him the carriage and the clumsy gait

of some lame animal or a three-legged Jew!
He pounded past in the mud and slush as if
his shabby boots were crushing dead men's bones—
hostile, rather than indifferent...

Then from the same hell came another, the same
eyes and beard and backbone, stick and rags—
nothing distinguished these centenarian twins
clumping identically toward an unknown goal.

Was it some vile conspiracy, or just
coincidence that made a fool of me?
To the seventh power—I counted every one—
this sinister ancient reproduced himself!

Doubtless to you my dread seems ludicrous,
unless a brotherly shudder lets you see:
for all their imminent decrepitude,
these seven monsters had eternal life!

I doubt if I could have survived an eighth
such apparition, father and son of himself,
inexorable Phoenix, loathsome avatar!
—I turned my back on the whole damned parade.

Indignant as a drunk who sees the world
double, I staggered home and locked my door,
scared and sick at heart and scandalized
that so much mystery could be absurd!

Vainly my reason sought to take the helm—
the gale made light of purpose, and my soul
went dancing on, an old and mastless scow
dancing across a black and shoreless sea.

93 ✱ THE LITTLE OLD WOMEN

to Victor Hugo

I

In murky corners of old cities where
everything—horror too—is magical,
I study, servile to my moods, the odd
and charming refuse of humanity.

These travesties were women once—Laïs
or Eponine! Love them, pathetic freaks,
hunchbacked and crippled—for they still have souls!
In ragged skirts and threadbare finery

they creep, tormented by the wicked gusts,
cowering each time an omnibus
thunders past, and clutching a reticule
as if it were a relic sewn with spells.

Whether they mince like marionettes or drag
themselves along like wounded animals,
they dance—against their will, the creatures dance—
sad bells on which a merciless Devil tugs.

They waver, but their eyes are gimlet-sharp
and gleam like holes where water sleeps at night—
the eyes of a child, a little girl who laughs
in sacred wonder at whatever shines!

—The coffins of old women are often the size
of a child's, have you ever noticed? Erudite
Death, by making the caskets match, suggests
a tidy symbol, if in dubious taste,

and when I glimpse one of these feeble ghosts
at grips with Paris and its murderous swarm,

it always seems to me the poor old thing
is slowly crawling toward a second crib;

or else those ill-assorted limbs propose
a problem in geometry: to fit
so many crooked corpses, how many times
must the workman alter a coffin's shape?

Those eyes are cisterns fed by a million tears,
or crucibles cracked by an ore that has gone cold:
irresistible their sovereignty
to one who suckled at disaster's dugs!

2

A Vestal at defunct *Frascati*'s shrine;
a priestess of Thalia whose memory survives
only in one long-dead prompter's mind;
the profligate of *Tivoli* in her prime;

this one a martyr to her fatherland,
that one her husband's victim, and one more
doomed by her son to a Madonna's grief—
all could make a river of their tears.

And all beguile me, but especially
those who, honeying their pain, implore
Addiction that had once lent them its wings:
"Mighty Hippogriff, let me fly again!"

3

Little old women! I remember one
I had trailed for hours, until the sky
went scarlet as a wound, and she sat down
lost in thought on a public-garden bench,

listening to the tunes our soldiers play—
brazen music for daylight's waning gold

(and yet such martial measures stir the soul,
granting a kind of glory to the crowd)...

Upright and proud she sat, and greedily
drank in the military airs, her eyes
like some old eagle's brightening beneath
the absent laurel on her marble brow!

4

And so you wander, stoic and inured
to all the uproar of the heedless town:
broken-hearted mothers, trollops, saints,
whose names were once the order of the day,

embodiments of glory and of grace!
Who knows you now? From doorways, derelicts
murmur obscene endearments as you pass,
and mocking children caper at your heels...

Poor wizened spooks, ashamed to be alive,
you hug the walls, sickly and timorous,
and no one greets you, no one says goodbye
to rubbish ready for eternity!

But I who at a distance follow you
and anxiously attend your failing steps
as if I had become your father—mine
are secret pleasures you cannot suspect!

I see first love in bloom upon your flesh,
dark or luminous I see your vanished days—
my teeming heart exults in all your sins
and all your virtues magnify my soul!

Flotsam, my family—ruins, my race!
Each night I offer you a last farewell!

Where will you be tomorrow, ancient Eves
under God's undeviating paw?

94 ✽ BLIND MEN

Consider them, my soul: how hideous!
Eerie as sleepwalkers, vaguely absurd
as dummies are—dummies that can walk,
blinking their useless lids at nothingness.

Their eyes are quenched, and yet they seem to stare
at something, somewhere, questioning the sky
and never bending their benighted heads
in reverie toward the cobblestones.

What difference between their infinite dark
and the eternal silence? Round us all,
meanwhile, the city sings, and laughs, and screams,

mad in pursuit of pleasure, whereas I...
I too drag by, but wonder, duller still,
what Heaven holds for them, all these blind men?

95 ✽ IN PASSING

The traffic roared around me, deafening!
Tall, slender, in mourning—noble grief—
a woman passed, and with a jeweled hand
gathered up her black embroidered hem;

stately yet lithe, as if a statue walked...
And trembling like a fool, I drank from eyes
as ashen as the clouds before a gale
the grace that beckons and the joy that kills.

Lightning...then darkness! Lovely fugitive
whose glance has brought me back to life! But where
is life—not this side of eternity?

Elsewhere! Too far, too late, or never at all!
Of me you know nothing, I nothing of you—you
who I might have loved and who knew that too!

96 ❋ SKELETON CREW

I

Colored plates from medical texts
peddled along these dusty quays
where corpses of so many books
rot in endlessly rifled graves,

illustrations that the skill
and rigor of a master hand
have made, however grim the theme,
incontrovertibly beautiful,

often—crowning horror!—display
anatomical mannequins
all vein and muscle, or skeletons
digging, bone on naked bone.

2

Helots of the charnel-house,
submissive and macabre drones,
can all your anguished vertebrae
or those espaliered arteries

reveal what preternatural crop
you wrest from the reluctant earth,

and tell which farmer's granary
your labors are condemned to fill?

Hard emblem of explicit fate,
would you declare by this device
that even in the sepulchre
our promised sleep will be denied?

that Nothingness has played us false,
that even Death is a deceit,
and that throughout eternity
we are intended, after all,

to scrape the unavailing soil
of some forsaken wilderness,
and drive again the heavy spade
under our bare and bleeding foot?

97 ❈ TWILIGHT: EVENING

It comes as an accomplice, stealthily,
the lovely hour that is the felon's friend;
the sky, like curtains round a bed, draws close,
and man prepares to become a beast of prey.

Longed for by those whose aching arms confess:
we earned our daily bread, at last it comes,
evening and the anodyne it brings
to workmen free to sleep and dream of sleep,
to stubborn scholars puzzling over texts,
to minds consumed by one tormenting pain...
Meantime, foul demons in the atmosphere
dutifully waken—they have work to do—
rattling shutters as they take the sky.
Under the gas lamps shaken by that wind
whoredom invades and everywhere at once
debauches on invisible thoroughfares,

as if the enemy had launched a raid;
it fidgets like a worm in the city's filth,
filching its portion of Man's daily bread.

Listen! Now you can hear the kitchens hiss,
the stages yelp, the music drown it all!
The dens that specialize in gambling fill
with trollops and their vague confederates,
and thieves untroubled by a second thought
will soon be hard at work (they also serve)
softly forcing doors and secret drawers
to dress their sluts and live a few days more.

This is the hour to compose yourself, my soul;
ignore the noise they make; avert your eyes.
Now comes the time when invalids grow worse
and darkness takes them by the throat; they end
their fate in the usual way, and all their sighs
turn hospitals into caves of the winds.
More than one will not come back for broth
warmed at the fireside by devoted hands.

Most of them, in fact, have never known
a hearth to come to, and have never lived.

98 ❀ GAMBLERS

They sit in shabby armchairs, ancient whores
with eyebrows painted over pitiless eyes,
simpering so that the garish gems they wear
jiggle at their withered powdered ears.

Around the green felt, lipless faces loom
or colorless lips and toothless jaws, above
feverish fingers that cannot lie still
but fumble in empty pockets, trembling breasts;

under the dirty ceilings and a row
of dusty chandeliers, the low-hung lamps
sway over famous poets' shadowed brows,
the sweat of which they come to squander here;

this hideous pageant passed before my eyes
as if a nightmare picked out each detail:
I saw myself in a corner of that hushed den
watching it all, cold, mute—and envious!

envying the stubborn passion of such men,
the deadly gaiety of those old whores—
all blithely trafficking, as I looked on,
in honor or beauty—whatever they could sell!

Horrible, that I should envy these
who rush so recklessly into the pit,
each in his frenzy ravenous to prefer
pain to death, and hell to nothingness!

99 ✻ DANCE OF DEATH

Proud of her height as if she were alive,
she manages her props—her huge bouquet,
her scarf, her gloves—with all the unconcern—
or is it the disdain?—of a practiced flirt.

Who ever saw a wasp with a waist like that!
Or so many yards of gown so readily
gathered up to show a wizened foot
crammed into its crimson satin shoe?

The frill that runs along her clavicle
as if a stream caressed the stones in its bed
demurely screens from idle scrutiny
the deadly charms she *will* keep in the dark.

Those shadows are the making of her eyes,
and the braid of buds around her nodding brow
is not so neatly plaited as her spine—
O lure of Nothingness so well tricked out!

Drunk on flesh, young lovers libel you
a caricature—they cannot understand
the beauty of your true embodiment:
Skeleton, you suit me down to the ground,

as grinning from ear to absent ear you come
to spoil the Feast, or cannot keep away
because some hunger in the marrow of your bones
compels you to our human carnival...

Will music and the flaring lights beguile
a mocking nightmare you cannot escape?
Is it the torrent of orgies you require
to douse the hellfire kindled in your heart?

Inexhaustible pit of folly and sin!
Eternal alembic of the ancient pain!
Threading the twisted trellis of your ribs
the insatiable worm, I see, is still at work!

To tell the truth, I fear your coquetry
will fail to find the victims it deserves:
which of these mortal hearts can take your jokes?
The charms of Dread are not for everyone.

What visions cloud the chasm of your eyes?
Even the bravest partner joins the dance
with a twinge of terror as he contemplates
the eternal smile of thirty-two white teeth!

Yet who has not embraced a skeleton,
not eaten what the grave claims for its own?

What does the costume matter, or the scent?
"Disgusted"? All you show is your conceit!

Noseless camp-follower, irresistible drab,
disabuse these dancers of their airs:
"For all your skill with powder and with musk
each of you stinks to heaven—or hell—of death!

A withered Antinous here, his Emperor there,
equally worm-eaten, hoary belles and beaux—
the universal throb of the Dance of Death
drags you down to Whereabouts Unknown!

From Senegal to the cold quays of the Seine
the mortal swarm jigs on, ecstatic, blind
to the Angel's trumpet somewhere overhead,
gaping like a blackened blunderbuss...

Death in every latitude dotes on you
and your contortions, ludicrous Mankind,
and often, like you, daubing herself with myrrh,
mixes her scorn with your delirium!"

100 ✺ LOVE OF DECEIT

As you dance by, beloved indolence
—the music fading, though it fills the room—
you seem to hover in your listlessness,
and boredom glistens in your heavy glance;

while midnight's sconces imitate the dawn,
the gaslight touches up your chalky face
with an appalling luster of its own—
your eyes, as in a portrait, follow me,

and I muse: how lovely! how grotesquely young!
burdened as she is with memory's crown

and a heart that, bruised like a peach, must be
ripe as her body for the feast of love.

Are you the sovereign harvest of the fall?
Are you the savor of the Happy Isles?
—ultimate urn that bides its time for tears,
caressing pillow, or narcotic rose?

I know there are eyes, the saddest eyes of all,
that have no precious secrets to conceal,
spurious reliquaries proudly shown,
deeper, and emptier, than the skies themselves!

Save the appearances! Is it not enough
to thrill a heart that cannot bear the truth?
What if you are stupid or indifferent?
Mask or sham, your beauty I adore.

101 ❊ "I Have Not Forgotten..."

I have not forgotten the house we lived in then,
it was just outside of town, a little white house
in a skimpy grove that hid the naked limbs
of plaster goddesses—the Venus was chipped!
Nor those seemingly endless evenings when the sun
(whose rays ignited every windowpane)
seemed, like a wide eye in the wondering sky,
to contemplate our long silent meals,
kindling more richly than any candlelight
the cheap curtains and the much-laundered cloth.

102 ❊ "You Used to Be Jealous..."

You used to be jealous of our old nurse
who sleeps, warm heart and all, beneath the sod.
We ought to bring her flowers, even so.

The dead, poor things, have sorrows of their own,
and when October comes and strips the trees
and hums its dismal tune among the graves,
how thankless we the living must appear,
sleeping as we do in our own beds
while they, subsiding into black despair,
without a bedmate or a joke to share,
worm-eaten skeletons, old and cold, endure
the constant seeping of the winter snows,
the passage of the years, and not one soul
to change the withered wreaths on rusty grilles...

When the log I put on the fire hisses and sings,
if I should see her sitting there, quite still,
or if on some cold blue December night
I found her hovering in a corner of my room,
somehow escaping her eternal bed
to cast a motherly eye on her grownup child,
what could I find to say to this pious soul
as I watched the tears filling her hollow eyes?

103 ✸ MISTS AND RAINS

Waning autumn, winter, mud-bound spring—
I thank these somnolent seasons that I love
for offering to both my heart and mind
so vaporous a shroud, so vague a tomb.

Here on this huge plain where the wind perfects
a will of its own and the weather vane cries all night,
now and not in the tepid days to come
my soul prefers to spread her raven wings.

Filled with dead and dying things, the heart
itself is frozen fast, and best of all
—O queen of our climate, ashen time of year!—

livid shadows never seem to change
except on moonless nights when two by two
we rock our pain to sleep on a reckless bed.

104 ❀ PARISIAN DREAM

I

It is a terrible terrain
      no mortal eye has seen
whose image still seduces me
      this morning as it fades...

Sleep is full of miracles!
      Some impulse in my dream
had rid the region I devised
      of every growing thing,

and proud of the resulting scene
      I savored in my art
the rapturous monotony
      of metal, water, stone...

A maze of stairs and arches formed
      an endless palace filled
with basins where the bright cascades
      fell into tarnished gold;

Like crystal curtains, cataracts
      streamed down metal walls,
shimmering where the ripples
      made perpetual descent;

colonnades instead of trees
      shaded sleeping pools
where, vain as women, huge naiads
      marveled at themselves;

pale-blue sheets of water spread
        between the marble quays—
their rims of rose and green converged
        a universe away;

unimaginable gems
        glowed in magic streams;
mirrors dizzily exchanged
        the dazzling world they showed!

Sacred rivers crossed the sky
        in silent unconcern,
pouring the treasure of their urns
        into diamond gulfs.

Architect of such conceits,
        I sent submissive seas
into the jeweled conduits
        my will erected there;

and every color, even black,
        became a lustrous prism;
liquid turned to glowing glass
        and what was crystal flowed;

yet neither sun nor moon appeared,
        and no horizon paled
to light such wonders—from *within*
        each thing was luminous!

And on these marvels as they moved
        there weighed (without a sound—
the eye alone was master here)
        the silence of the Void.

2

Waking, dazzled, I was back
    in my familiar slum
and felt returning to my soul
    the curse of all my cares;

with unrelenting strokes the clock
    insisted it was noon,
and shadows poured out of the sky
    upon a sluggish world.

105 ✿ TWILIGHT: DAYBREAK

The morning wind rattles the windowpanes
and over the barracks reveille rings out.

Dreams come now, bad dreams, and teenage boys
burrow into their pillows. Now the lamp
that glowed at midnight seems, like a bloodshot eye,
to throb and throw a red stain on the room;
balked by the stubborn body's weight, the soul
mimics the lamplight's struggles with the dawn.
Like a face in tears—the tears effaced by wind—
the air is tremulous with escaping things,
and Man is tired of writing, Woman of love.

Here and there, chimneys begin to smoke.
Whores, mouths gaping, eyelids gray as ash,
sleep on their feet, leaning against the walls,
and beggar-women, hunched over sagging breasts,
blow on burning sticks, then on their hands.
Now, the hungry feel the cold the worst,
and women in labor suffer the sharpest pains;
now, like a sob cut short by a clot of blood,
a rooster crows somewhere; a sea of mist
swirls around the buildings; in the Hôtel-Dieu

the dying breathe their last, while the debauched,
spent by their exertions, sleep alone.

Shivering dawn, in a wisp of pink and green,
totters slowly across the empty Seine,
and dingy Paris—old drudge rubbing its eyes—
picks up its tools to begin another day.

WINE

106 ❋ THE SOUL OF THE WINE

sang by night in its bottles: "Dear mankind—
dear and disinherited! Break the seal
of scarlet wax that darkens my glass jail,
and I shall bring you light and brotherhood!

How long you labored on the fiery hills
among the needful vines! I know it cost
fanatic toil to make me what I am,
and I shall not be thankless or malign:

I take a potent pleasure when I pour
down the gullet of a workingman,
and how much more I relish burial
in his hot belly than in my cold vaults!

Listen to my music after hours,
the hope that quickens in my throbbing heart;
lean on the table with your sleeves rolled up
and honor me: you will know happiness,

for I shall bring a gleam to your wife's eyes,
a glow of power to your son's wan cheeks
and for this athlete flagging in the race
shall be the oil that strengthens wrestlers' limbs.

Into you I shall flow, ambrosia brewed
from precious seed the eternal Sower cast,
so that the poetry born of our love will grow
and blossom like a flower in God's sight!"

107 ❋ RAGPICKERS' WINE

Look—there! in the streetlamp's dingy glow
—wind rattling the glass, lashing the flame—

out of the muddy labyrinth of streets
teeming with unruly, sordid types,

a ragpicker stumbles past, wagging his head
and bumping into walls with a poet's grace,
pouring out his heartfelt schemes to one
and all, including spies of the police.

He swears to wonders, lays down noble laws,
reforms the wicked, raises up their prey,
and under the lowering canopy of heaven
intoxicates himself on his own boasts.

More such creatures—who knows where they live?—
wracked by drudgery, ruined by the years,
staggering under enormous sacks of junk
—the vomit of surfeited Paris—now appear,

whole armies of them, reeking of sour wine,
comrades in arms, whitened by their wars,
whiskers drooping like surrendered flags...
Before them wave the banners and the palms—

as if by magic, arches of triumph rise
and in the chaos of exploding flares,
bugle calls and battle cries and drums,
they march in glory past a cheering mob!

So it is, through frivolous mankind,
that wine like a bright Pactolus pours its gold;
with human tongues it glorifies its deeds
and rules by what it gives, as true kings do.

To drown the spleen and pacify the sloth
of these old wrecks who die without a word,
God, taking pity, created Sleep; to which
Man added Wine, the sun's anointed son!

108 ❋ THE MURDERER'S WINE

My wife is dead, so now I'm free
    to drink until I drop.
No more nagging when I'm broke—
    I put a stop to that.

Today I'm happy. What a day—
    not a cloud in the sky!
The summer must have been this hot
    when I was courting her.

Thirsty—I'm thirsty all the time!
    A drink is what I need,
wine enough to fill her grave...
    which means a lot of wine.

You see, I threw her down a well
    and afterward pushed in
the flagstones piled around the edge—
    that ought to keep her still.

"Meet me after dark," I begged,
    "where we can be alone"—
the right words came all by themselves,
    you don't forget such tunes.

I told her we could patch things up
    the way they used to be,
and she...believed me! Women are
    crazy. Men are too.

Even though her face was lined
    she hadn't lost her looks,
and I still—I loved her too much;
    that's why she had to die.

Nobody understands. Name one
    of the numbskull drunks I know
who ever dreamed when nights went bad
    that wine could make a shroud.

That bunch! They feel about as much
    as plowshares breaking ground—
plow or harrow! which of them
    has ever known True Love

with all its cavalcade of tears
    and fears and broken hearts
and poison darts and rattling chains…
    and now the rattling bones?

I'm free of that—free and alone!
    Tonight I'll be dead drunk
and lay myself out on the ground
    without a second thought;

I'll sleep like a dog and never know
    or care when the skidding wheels
of a wagon loaded down with rocks
    crushes my guilty head

or cuts my heedless guts in half—
    what happens, after that,
is no concern of mine: to Hell
    with Hell! Good riddance, God!

109 ❋ THE SOLITARY'S WINE

The unexampled ogle of a whore
glinting toward you like the silver ray
the wavering moon releases on the lake
when she would bathe her listless beauty there;

the final bag of coins in a gambler's fist;
the cavernous kisses you get from Adeline;
the maddening tune that will not let you go,
as if it echoed faintly all of human pain—

none of that, my Bottle, can compare
with the remedy your long green curves supply
to the worshipful poet's ever-thirsting heart;

for him you pour out hope and youth and life—
and pride, the beggars' treasure! give us pride
that makes us winners—we shall be as gods!

110 ❋ LOVERS' WINE

Today the air is splendid!
no need for bridle or spurs—
mount the wine and set off
for a sky that is magic—divine!

Like a pair of angels driven
by some implacable fever,
up into morning's blue crystal
to follow the far mirage!

Cradled gently on the wing
of the conniving whirlwind,
rapt in a parallel transport,

my sister, we shall flee
side by side, unflagging,
to the Paradise of my dreams!

FLOWERS OF EVIL

III ❀ DESTRUCTION

I come and go—the Demon tags along,
hanging around me like the air I breathe;
each time I swallow he fills my burning lungs
with sinful cravings never satisfied.

Sometimes (for he knows my love of Art)
he visits in a seductive woman's form
and with the specious alibis of despair
inures my lips to squalid appetites.

Thereby he leads me out of God's regard,
spent and gasping—out to where the vast
barrens of Boredom stretch infinitely,

and here he hurls into my startled face
the open wounds, the rags they have soaked
through, and all Destruction's bloody bag of tricks!

112 ❀ A MARTYR

DRAWING BY AN UNKNOWN MASTER

Among decanters, ivories and gems,
    sumptuous divans
with gold-brocaded silks and fragrant gowns
    trailing languid folds,

where lilies sorrowing in crystal urns
    exhale their final sigh
and where, as if the room were under glass,
    the air is pestilent,

a headless corpse emits a stream of blood
    the sopping pillows shed

onto thirsty sheets that drink it up
    as greedily as sand.

Pale as the visions that our captive eyes
    discover in the dark,
the head, enveloped in its somber mane,
    emeralds still in its ears,

watches from a stool, a thing apart,
    and from the eyes rolled back
to whiteness blank as daybreak emanates
    an alabaster stare.

The carcass sprawling naked on the bed
    displays without a qualm
the splendid cynosure that prodigal
    Nature bestowed—betrayed;

pink with gold clocks, one stocking clings—
    a souvenir, it seems;
the garter, gleaming like a secret eye,
    darts a jeweled glance.

Doubled by a full-length portrait drawn
    in the same provocative pose,
the strange demeanor of this solitude
    reveals love's darker side—

profligate practices and guilty joys,
    embraces bound to please
the swarm of naughty angels frolicking
    in the curtains overhead;

yet judging from the narrow elegance
    of her shoulders sloping down
past the serpentine curve of her waist
    to the almost bony hips,

she still is young!—What torment in her soul,
     what tedium that stung
her senses gave this body to the throng
     of wandering, lost desires?

In spite of so much love, did the vengeful man
     she could not, living, sate
assuage on her inert and docile flesh
     the measure of his lust?

And did he, gripping her blood-stiffened hair,
     lift up that dripping head
and press on her cold teeth one final kiss?
     The sullied corpse is still.

—Far from a scornful world of jeering crowds
     and peering magistrates,
sleep in peace, lovely enigma, sleep
     in your mysterious tomb:

your bridegroom roves, and your immortal form
     keeps vigil when he sleeps;
like you, no doubt, he will be constant too,
     and faithful unto death.

113 ✻ LESBOS

Mother of Latin games and Greek delights,
Lesbos! where the kisses, languid or rapt,
cool as melons, burning as the sun,
adorn the dark and gild the shining days
given to Latin games and Greek delights;

Lesbos, where the kisses, like cascades,
teeming and turbulent yet secret, deep,
plunge undaunted into unplumbed gulfs

and gather there, gurgling and sobbing till
they overflow in ever-new cascades!

Where Phryne's breasts are judged by her own kind
and every sigh is answered by a kiss;
where Aphrodite envies Sappho's rite
at shrines as favored as the Cyprian's own,
and Phryne's judges are never unkind;

Lesbos, where on suffocating nights
before their mirrors girls with hollow eyes
caress their ripened limbs in sterile joy
and taste the fruit of their nubility
on Lesbos during suffocating nights!

What if old Plato's scowling eyes condemn?
Kisses absolve you by their sweet excess
whose subtleties are inexhaustible!
Queen of the tender Archipelago,
pursue what Plato's scowling eyes condemn

and win your pardon for the martyrdom
forever inflicted on ambitious hearts
that yearn, far from us, for a radiant smile
they dimly glimpse on the rim of other skies—
you win your pardon for that martyrdom!

Which of the Gods will dare to disapprove
and chide the pallor of your studious brow?
Until Olympian scales have weighed the flood
of tears your rivers pour into the sea,
which of the Gods will dare to disapprove?

What use to us are laws of right and wrong?
High-hearted virgins, honor of the Isles,
your altars are august as any: love
will laugh at Heaven as it laughs at Hell!
What use to us are laws of right and wrong?

For Lesbos has chosen me among all men
to sing the secrets of her budding grove;
from childhood I have shared the mystery
of frenzied laughter laced with sullen tears,
and therefore am I chosen among men

to keep my lookout high on Sappho's Cliff,
vigilant as a sleepless sentinel
gazing night and day for the barque or brig
whose distant outline shimmers on the blue;
I keep my lookout high on Sappho's Cliff

to discover if the sea is merciful
and if, out of the sobbing breakers' surge,
there will return to Lesbos, which forgives,
the cherished corpse of Sappho who left us
to discover if the sea is merciful—

of virile Sappho, the lover and the poet,
fairer than Aphrodite whose blue gaze
surrenders to the somber radiance
of ash-encircled burning eyes—
the eyes of virile Sappho, the lover and the poet!

Fairer than the Anadyómene
scattering her bright serenity
and all the treasures of her golden youth
upon old Ocean dazzled by his child—
fairer than the Anadyómene

was Sappho on the day she broke her vow
and died apostate to her own command,
her lovely body forfeit to a brute
whose arrogance avenged the sacrilege
of Sappho, lost the day she broke her vow...

And from that time to this, Lesbos laments.
Heedless of the homage of the world,
she drugs herself each night with cries of pain
that rend the skies above her empty shores,
and from that time to this Lesbos laments!

114 ❋ DAMNED WOMEN

DELPHINE AND HIPPOLYTA

Disclosed, though dimly, by the faltering lamps,
Hippolyta rested on a soft and scented couch
reliving those caresses that had raised
the curtains of her inexperience.

Wild-eyed after the storm, she conjured up
already-distant skies of innocence,
just as a traveler might turn back to glimpse
blue horizons lost with the morning's light.

The sluggish tears of her unfocussed gaze,
her eager arms flung down as in defeat—
every trace of voluptuous apathy
served and set off her fragile loveliness.

Reclining at her feet, elated yet calm,
Delphine stared up at her with shining eyes
the way a lioness will watch her prey
once her fangs have marked it for her own.

In all her pride the potent beauty knelt
before the pitiable one, complacently
savoring the wine of her triumph, reaching up
as though to garner fond acknowledgment.

She searched her victim's eyes for evidence
of the silent canticle that pleasure sings

and that sublime and infinite gratitude
that glistens under the eyelids like a sigh.

"Hippolyta, my angel, how do you feel now?
Surely you realize you must not grant
the holy sacrifice of your first bloom
to cruel gales that would disfigure it...

My kisses are as light as those mayflies
that graze the great transparent lakes at sunset;
his would trace their furrows on your flesh
like the tongue of some lacerating plow—

as if you had been trampled by a team
of oxen with inexorable hooves...
Hippolyta, sister! turn your face to me,
my heart and soul, my other half, my all!

Let me see your eyes, my heaven, my stars!
For one of their healing glances I shall trade
as yet untasted pleasures: you will drift
to sleep in my arms dreaming an endless dream!"

But then Hippolyta looked up: "Delphine,
I am grateful to you, I have no regrets,
yet I am troubled and my nerves are tense,
as if a dreadful feast had fouled the night...

Pangs of dread oppress me—I see ghosts
in black battalions beckoning me down
uncertain roads where each horizon ends
abruptly in a sky the color of blood.

What have we done—is it some wicked thing?
Must I endure this turmoil and this fear?
I cringe each time you call me 'angel,' yet
I feel my mouth long for you. No, Delphine—

don't look at me like that! I love you now
and I shall love you always: I choose you,
even if my choice becomes a trap
laid for me, and the onset of my doom."

With adamant eyes and a despotic voice,
Delphine replied, shaking her tragic mane
as if she stirred on the priestess's tripod:
"Who in love's name dares to speak of Hell?

My curse forever on the dreaming fool
who entered first that endless labyrinth
and tried for all his folly to enlist
love in the service of morality!

Whoever hopes to force into accord
day and darkness, shadow and radiance,
will never warm his vacillating flesh
in that red sun our bodies know as love!

Go now—go find yourself some stupid boy
and give his lust your virgin heart to maul;
then, filled with horror, livid with disgust,
bring back to me your mutilated breasts...

You cannot please two masters in this world!"
But then the girl, in a paroxysm of grief,
suddenly cried out: "There is emptiness
inside me—and that emptiness is my heart!

Searing as lava, deeper than the Void!
Nothing will satiate this monster's greed,
nothing appease the Fury who puts out
her flaming torch within my very blood...

O draw the curtains—leave the world outside!
There must be rest for all this weariness.

Let me annihilate myself upon
your breast and find the solace of a grave!"

Downward, wretched victims! ever down
the path you follow: make your way to hell,
into the pit where crime arouses crime,
seething together in the thunder's maw

and scourged by winds that never knew the sky
Down, frantic shades, and fall to your desires
where passion never slakes its raging thirst,
and from your pleasure stems your punishment.

Crack by crevice, into your sunless caves
feverish miasmas seep and gather strength
until they catch on fire like spirit lamps,
imbuing your bodies with their vile perfume.

The harsh sterility of your delight
scalds your throat and desiccates your skin—
and the eyeless cyclone of concupiscence
rattles your flesh like an abandoned flag.

Wandering far from all mankind, condemned
to forage in the wilderness like wolves,
pursue your fate, chaotic souls, and flee
the infinite you bear within yourselves!

115 ✻ DAMNED WOMEN

Pensive as cattle resting on the beach,
they are staring out to sea; their hands and feet
creep toward each other imperceptibly
and touch at last, hesitant then fierce.

How eagerly some, beguiled by secrets shared,
follow a talkative stream among the trees,

spelling out their timid childhood's love
and carving initials in the tender wood;

others pace as slow and grave as nuns
among the rocks where Anthony beheld
the purple breasts of his temptations rise
like lava from the visionary earth;

some by torchlight in the silent caves
consecrated once to pagan rites
invoke—to quench their fever's holocaust—
Bacchus, healer of the old regrets;

others still, beneath their scapulars,
conceal a whip that in the solitude
and darkness of the forest reconciles
tears of pleasure with the tears of pain.

Virgins, demons, monsters, martyrs, all
great spirits scornful of reality,
saints and satyrs in search of the infinite,
racked with sobs or loud in ecstasy,

you who my soul has followed to your hell,
Sisters! I love you as I pity you
for your bleak sorrows, for your unslaked thirsts,
and for the love that gorges your great hearts!

116 ❋ THE TWO KIND SISTERS

Death and Debauch, two friendly girls, bestow
lavish kisses, being in lusty health;
in years of labor, their still-virgin wombs,
covered with rags, have never given birth!

Notably for the poet—hell's own pet,
ominous enemy of the household gods—

whorehouse and charnel-house alike reserve
a bed Remorse has never visited.

Alcove and Coffin, rich in blasphemies,
with sisterly solicitude propose
terrible pleasures and appalling treats...

When will you bury me, Debauch? O Death,
whose pleasures rival hers, when will you come
to graft your cypress on her gruesome rose?

117 ✳ THE FOUNTAIN OF BLOOD

Sometimes I feel my blood is spilling out
in sobs, the way a fountain overflows.
I know I hear it, sighing as it goes,
and search my flesh, but cannot find the wound;

it turns the stones to archipelagoes,
as if the city were a battleground,
slaking the thirst of every living thing
and dyeing all the world of nature red.

How often have I called for wine to drug,
if only for a day, this wasting fear—
my ears grow sharp on wine, my eyes grow clear!

In love I've sought an hour's oblivion—
but love to me is a pallet stuffed with pins
that drains away my blood for whores to drink!

118 ✳ ALLEGORY

It is a lovely woman, richly dressed,
who shares her wineglass with her own long hair;
the brothel's rotgut and the brawls of love

121

have left the marble of her skin unmarred.
She flouts Debauchery and flirts with Death,
monsters who maim what they do not mow down,
and yet their talons have not dared molest
the simple majesty of this proud flesh.
Artemis walking, a sultana prone,
she worships pleasure with a Muslim's faith
and summons to her breasts with open arms
the race of men enslaved by her warm eyes.
Sterile this virgin, yet imperative
to the world and its workings what she knows:
the body's beauty is a noble gift
that wrests a pardon for all infamy.
What is Purgatory, what is Hell
to her? When she must go into the Night,
her eyes will gaze upon the face of Death
without hate, without remorse—as one newborn.

119 ✳ EVEN SHE WHO WAS CALLED BEATRICE
BY MANY WHO KNEW NOT WHEREFORE

Wandering a wasteland at high noon
where only ashes echoed my lament
to leafless nature, whetting as I went
the dagger of my mind against my heart,
I saw a dismal storm cloud bearing down
upon my head, bristling with vicious imps
as cruel as they were inquisitive.
Coldly they began to stare, the way
people with nothing better to do will mock
and marvel at a madman, these would laugh,
nudging each other and exchanging winks,
and whisper (loud enough for me to hear):

"Take a good look at this caricature
of Hamlet or—with his disheveled hair,
his indecisive gaze—of Hamlet's Ghost!

Who could keep from laughing at the sight—
this shabby aesthete, this artistic sham,
this ham, this clamorous comedian
who knowing his abracadabra inside out
attempts to interest eagles (crickets too),
even flowers and fountains in his ranted woes,
reciting his routine at the top of his lungs
to us as well, who hatched the whole damned thing!"

I might (my pride is mountainous—a match
for clouds and crowds of demons and their jeers)
have simply turned away and wandered past,
had I not seen among that nasty crew
—nor was the sun unsettled by this crime—
the queen of my heart (I recognized those eyes)
laughing at my pain with all the rest
and giving them now and then a filthy kiss.

120 ❋ Metamorphoses of the Vampire

The woman, meanwhile, writhing like a snake
across hot coals and hiking up her breasts
over her corset stays, began to speak
as if her mouth had steeped each word in musk:
"My lips are smooth, and with them I know how
to smother conscience somewhere in these sheets.
I make the old men laugh like little boys,
and on my triumphant bosom all tears dry.

Look at me naked, and I will replace
sun and moon and every star in the sky.
So apt am I, dear scholar, in my lore
that once I fold a man in these fatal arms
or forfeit to his teeth my breasts, which are
timid and teasing, tender and tyrannous,
upon these cushions swooning with delight
the impotent angels would be damned for me!"

When she had sucked the marrow from my bones,
and I leaned toward her listlessly
to return her loving kisses, all I saw
was a kind of slimy wineskin brimming with pus!
I closed my eyes in a spasm of cold fear,
and when I opened them to the light of day,
beside me, instead of that potent mannequin
who seemed to have drunk so deeply of my blood,
there trembled the wreckage of a skeleton
that grated with the cry of a weather vane
or a rusty signboard hanging from a pole,
battered by the wind on winter nights.

121 ✳ A VOYAGE TO CYTHERA

My heart flew up like a bird before the mast,
circled the shrouds and mounted free and clear;
the ship rolled on beneath a cloudless sky
like an angel drunk on the glory of the sun.

What is that dreary island—the black one there?
Cythera, someone says, the one in the song

insipid Eldorado of good old boys:
it isn't much of a place, as you can see.

Island of feasting hearts and secret joys!
Like a fragrance, the voluptuary ghost
of Aphrodite floats above your shores,
inflaming minds with languor and with love.

Island green with myrtle, rich with bloom,
revered forever by all mortal men
from whose adoring hearts wells up a sigh
soft as the fallen petals of a rose

or the relentless moan of doves...Cythera now
was nothing more than a thistled promontory
vexed by the wheeling gulls' unruly cries.
Yet there was something...I could see it now;

no temple sheltered by its sacred grove,
no priestess gathering blossoms, her loose robe
half-opened to the breezes as they passed,
her flesh ignited by a secret fire;

but as we cleared the coastline—close enough
to scare the shorebirds with our flapping sails—
we saw what it was: black against the sky,
no cypress but a branching gallows-tree.

Perched on their provender, ferocious birds
were ravaging the ripe corpse hanging there,
driving their filthy beaks like cruel drills
into each cranny of its rotten flesh;

the eyes were holes, and from the ruined groin
a coil of heavy guts had tumbled out—
the greedy creatures, gorged on hideous sweets,
had peck by vicious peck castrated him.

Below his feet, among a whining pack
that waited, muzzles lifted for their share,
some bigger beast was prowling back and forth
like a hangman huge among his underlings.

Inhabitant of Cythera, rapture's child,
how silently you suffered these affronts
in expiation of your shameful rites
and sins that have proscribed your burial.

Ludicrous carcass! I hung there with you,
and at the sight of your insulted limbs

I tasted, like vomit in my mouth,
the bitter tide of age-old sufferings.

Knowing what you were and what you are,
I felt each saber tooth and jabbing beak
of jet-black panthers and of carrion-crows
that once so loved to lacerate my flesh.

... The sky was suave, the sea serene; for me
from now on everything was bloody and black
—the worse for me—and as if in a shroud
my heart lay buried in this allegory.

On Aphrodite's island all I found
was a token gallows where my image hung...
Lord give me strength and courage to behold
my body and my heart without disgust!

122 ❋ Eros and the Skull

AN OLD COLOPHON

Insolent Eros,
        seated on the skull
        of Humanity
        as if on a throne,
gaily blows bubbles:
        they rise, one after
        another, as if
        to rejoin the worlds
in the stratosphere.
        Frail and luminous,
        each globe as it mounts
        explodes, spattering
its tenuous soul
        like a golden dream.
        I hear the skull moan
        as each one shatters:

"When will this callous,
     ridiculous game
     of yours be over?
     What your cruel breath
scatters into air,
     Monster Murderer,
     is my very flesh
     and blood—gray matters!"

REBELLION

123 ❀ SAINT PETER'S DENIAL

The tide of curses day by day ascends
unto His hosts—and God, what does He do?
Like a tyrant gorged on meat and wine, He sleeps—
the sound of our blasphemies sweet in His Ears.

The martyrs' sobs, the screaming at the stake
compose, no doubt, a heady symphony;
indeed, for all the blood their pleasure costs,
the Heavens have not yet had half enough!

Remember the Mount of Olives, Jesus? When
you fell on your knees and humbly prayed to Him
Who laughed on high at the sound of hammering
as the butchers drove the nails into your flesh?

And when they spat on your divinity,
the jeering scullions and the conscript scum—
that moment when you felt the thorns impale
the skull that housed Humanity itself;

when the intolerable weight of your tormented flesh
hung from your distended arms; when blood
and sweat cascaded from your whitening brow;
when you were made a target for all eyes—

did you dream then of the wonder-working days
when you came to keep eternal promises,
riding an ass, and everywhere the ways
strewn with palms and flowers—those were the days!

when, your heart on fire with valor and with hope,
you whipped the moneylenders out of that place—
you were master then! But now, has not remorse
pierced your side even deeper than the spear?

Myself, I shall be satisfied to quit
a world where action is no kin to dreams;
would I had used—and perished by—the sword!
Peter denied his Master...He did well!

124 ❋ ABEL AND CAIN

I

Race of Abel, sleep and feed,
God is pleased;

grovel in the dirt and die,
Race of Cain.

Race of Abel, your sacrifice
flatters the nostrils of the Seraphim;

Race of Cain, is your punishment
never to know an end?

Race of Abel, your fields prosper,
your cattle grow fat;

Race of Cain, your belly clamors
like a famished dog.

Race of Abel, warm yourself
at the hearth of your fathers;

shiver in the jackal's den,
Race of Cain.

Race of Abel, increase and multiply,
even your gold will breed;

though your heart burn, Race of Cain,
beware great appetites.

Race of Abel, build your cities
even as the ants;

Race of Cain, your children beg
for bread beside the road.

2

Race of Abel, your corpse
will fatten the reeking earth;

your labor, Race of Cain,
is not yet done.

Race of Abel, behold your shame:
the sword yields to the butcher knife!

Rise up, Race of Cain,
and cast God down upon the earth!

125 ✽ SATAN'S LITANIES

Aptest angel and the loveliest!
a God betrayed, to whom no anthems rise,
    Satan, take pity on my sore distress!
Prince of exiles, exiled Prince who, wronged,
yet rises ever stronger from defeat,
    Satan, take pity on my sore distress!
Omniscient ruler of the hidden realm,
patient healer of all human pain,
    Satan, take pity on my sore distress!
Who even to lepers and such outcast scum
by love inculcates all we know of bliss,
    Satan, take pity on my sore distress!

Who gave to Death, your oldest paramour,
a child both lunatic and lovely—Hope!
    Satan, take pity on my sore distress!
Who grants the criminal's last look of pride
that damns the crowd beneath the guillotine,
    Satan, take pity on my sore distress!
Who knows each cranny in the grudging earth
where gems are hidden by a jealous God,
    Satan, take pity on my sore distress!
Whose eye can pierce the deepest arsenal
where buried metals slumber in the dark,
    Satan, take pity on my sore distress!
Within whose mighty arm the sleepwalker
avoids the rooftop's yawning precipice,
    Satan, take pity on my sore distress!
Who magically rescues the old bones
of drunkards trampled by the horses' hooves,
    Satan, take pity on my sore distress!
Who to console our sufferings has taught
how readily shot and powder may be mixed,
    Satan, take pity on my sore distress!
Who sets your sign, in sly complicity,
upon the rich man's unrelenting brow,
    Satan, take pity on my sore distress!
Who lights in women's greedy hearts and eyes
worship of wounds, rapacity for rags,
    Satan, take pity on my sore distress!
The outlaw's staff and the inventor's lamp,
confessor to the traitor, hanged man's priest,
    Satan, take pity on my sore distress!
Adoptive father to those an angry God
the Father drove from His earthly paradise,
    Satan, take pity on my sore distress!

PRAYER

Satan be praised! Glory to you on High
where once you reigned in Heaven, and in the Pit

where now you dream in taciturn defeat!
Grant that my soul, one day, beneath the Tree
of Knowledge, meet you when above your brow
its branches, like a second Temple, spread!

DEATH

126 ❋ THE DEATH OF LOVERS

We shall have richly scented beds—
couches deep as graves, and rare
flowers on the shelves will bloom
for us beneath a lovelier sky.

Emulously spending their last
warmth, our hearts will be as two
torches reflecting their double fires
in the twin mirrors of our minds.

One evening, rose and mystic blue,
we shall exchange a single glance,
a long sigh heavy with farewells;

and then an Angel, unlocking doors,
will come, loyal and gay, to bring
the tarnished mirrors back to life.

127 ❋ THE DEATH OF THE POOR

What else consoles? It is the remedy
and the preventive too, the one escape
that like a stupefying draught of wine
gives us the heart to get through one more day;

sure on the dim horizon shines one light
that never fails, in spite of storm and cold—
the famous inn all guidebooks recommend
where we can count on lodging for the Night.

Angel of Death, in your transforming hands
the straw we lie on turns to softest down,
our sleep is sound, our dreams are ecstasy!

Here is the mystic granary of heaven,
purse of the poor and our inheritance,
the open gateway to the unknown God!

128 ❋ THE DEATH OF ARTISTS

How often, grim Caricature, must I
jingle my bells and kiss your bestial brow?
Until my aim is true—the circle squared—
how many arrows forfeit to the Void?

We rack our brains with subtle stratagems
and ruin many massive armatures
before the splendid Creature may be seen
for whom our fatal longing makes us sob!

To some their idol will not be revealed,
and these doomed sculptors, branded with disgrace,
upbraid themselves and lacerate their breasts,

nursing one hope, sepulchral Capitol!—
that Death as it fills the sky like another sun
will make the flowers of their devising bloom!

129 ❋ DAY'S END

Mindless of the fading light,
Life—insolent, noisy Life—
squanders itself until night
voluptuously reaches for

the horizon, consoling all,
even hunger—concealing all,
even shame—and then the Poet
murmurs to himself: "At last!

Spine and spirit crave their rest
with one accord; my heart brims
over with dreams of dying—

I shall lie down, I shall sleep.
Shroud me in your panoply,
O replenishing darkness!"

130 ❀ A STRANGE MAN'S DREAM

to Nadar

Have you felt—I have—a pain that you enjoyed?
Do they say about you, too: "How strange he is!"
—I was dying, and a special agony
filled my eager soul: dread and desire,

anguish and expectation—no sense of revolt.
The closer I came to what would be the end,
the sharper was my torment and the more welcome;
my heart was wrenching free from the usual world.

I was like a child in front of a stage,
hating the curtain as if it were in the way...
Finally the cold truth was revealed:

I had simply died, and the terrible dawn
enveloped me. Could this be all there is?
The curtain was up, and I was waiting still.

131 ❋ TRAVELERS

to Maxime Du Camp

I

The child enthralled by lithographs and maps
can satisfy his hunger for the world:
how limitless it is beneath the lamp,
and how it shrinks in the eyes of memory!

One morning we set out. Our heart is full,
our mind ablaze with rancor and disgust—
we yield it all to the rhythm of the waves,
our infinite self awash on the finite sea:

some are escaping from their country's shame,
some from the horror of life at home, and some
—astrologers blinded by a woman's stare—
are fugitives from Circe's tyranny;

rather than be turned to swine they drug
themselves on wind and sea and glowing skies;
rain and snow and incinerating suns
gradually erase her kisses' scars.

But only those who leave for leaving's sake
are *travelers*; hearts tugging like balloons,
they never balk at what they call their fate
and, not knowing why, keep muttering "Away!"

those whose longings have the shape of clouds,
who dream—as conscripts dream of guns—of huge
and fluctuating and obscure delights,
none of which has ever had a name.

2

As if we wanted to be a ball or a top!
bouncing and twirling—even in our sleep
we look for something, driven round and round
like a sun some cruel Angel spins in space.

Preposterous quest! whose goal cannot be known
but, being nowhere, can be anywhere;
only our hope is inexhaustible,
and Man pursues repose until he drops!

Our soul is a schooner seeking a free port,
and when the question rises from the deck,
a voice from the topmast eagerly replies:
"Happiness!...Glory!...Love!..." Another reef.

The lookout hails each island, after dark,
as El Dorado and the Promised Land;
imagination readies for its feast—
and sights a sandbar by the morning light.

Irons or overboard with the drunken tar,
pathetic lover of chimerical coasts
who dreams Atlantis and then finds the sea
emptier for one more fond mirage!

One more old sailor in the muddy slums
who meditates, half blind, on Happy Isles
and thinks he sees the beacons of Dakar
each time a candle gutters in the dark.

3

Awesome travelers! What noble chronicles
we read in your unfathomable eyes!
Open the sea-chests of your memories
and show us jewels made of storms and stars.

We long to journey without steam or sail!
Help us forget the prison of our days
and on the canvas of our minds unfurl
your visions framed by the horizon's gold.

Tell us what you've seen!

4

    "We've seen the stars,
the waves, and shoals we failed to see—we saw;
and though destruction came in many forms,
we were too often bored, the same as here.

The glory of the sun on Tyrian seas,
the glow of cities when the sun goes down,
awakened in our hearts a restless urge
to plunge into a still more distant sky.

None of the famous landscapes that we saw
equaled the mysterious allure
of those that Chance arranges in the clouds...
And our desire would let us have no peace!

Enjoyment breeds desire tenfold...Desire!
Old tree manured by pleasure, all the while
your bark will coarsen, growing thick and hard,
your branches seek the sun at closer range!

Great tree, will you grow forever, hardier
than the cypress? All the same, we've brought
these images for your albums, stay-at-homes
who prize whatever comes from far away:

idols we saw, hideous gods whose thrones
were set with emeralds the size of plums;
and palaces of marble lace whose cost
would ruin your most reckless millionaires;

robes embroidered by a thousand slaves;
women who filed their lacquered teeth to points;
jugglers sinuous as the snakes they charmed..."

5

Yes, and what else?

6

                "You talk just like a child!
Chief among all the wonders that we glimpsed
in every hole and corner, forced on our sight
at every turn of Fortune's fatal wheel—
the boring pageant of immortal sin:

Woman a slave and yet vainglorious,
stupid and unashamed in her self-love;
Man a greedy tyrant, slave of his slaves,
swelling the sewer to a stinking flood;

victims in tears, the hangman glorified;
the banquet seasoned and festooned with blood:
the poison of power clogs the despot's veins,
and the people kiss the knout that scourges them;

several religions similar to ours,
besieging heaven—the holy everywhere
like sybarites on rose-beds (only on
beds of nails) in hot pursuit of bliss;

Humanity enslaved by rhetoric
and mad today as it has ever been,
screaming to God in a tantrum of despair:
'I curse You in my Image—Father, be damned!'

And the least stupid, Ecstasy's elect,
fleeing the herd where Fate has penned them fast,

take refuge in the wards of Opium!
—So much for what is news around the world!"

7

It is a bitter truth our travels teach!
Tiny and monotonous, the world
has shown—will always show us—what we are:
oases of fear in the wasteland of ennui!

Choose your desolation—stay if you can,
stir if you must. One man chooses sloth
to cheat a tireless adversary, Time,
out of his triumph in the funeral games.

Another journeys, like the Wandering Jew,
forever, but no roving can evade
the merciless net; still others seem to know
how to kill Time before they're even weaned!

Yet we are his in the end. One hope remains:
to venture forth, with "Onward!" as our cry...
Just as once we set sail for Cathay,
wind in our hair, eyes on the open sea,

we shall embark upon the Sea of Shades
with all the elation of a boy's first cruise...
Do you hear those lovely voices? They have death
in their appeal: "Come with us, come and eat

the fragrant Lotus! Here is where we reap
the magic harvest that you hunger for!
Come and revel in the sweet delight
of days where it is always afternoon!"

Pylades is there, his arms held out;
we know the sound by heart, we guess the ghost!
It is her voice—we used to kiss her knees—
"Orestes, come—Electra waits for you..."

8

Death, old admiral, up anchor now,
this country wearies us. Put out to sea!
What if the waves and winds are black as ink,
our hearts are filled with light. You know our hearts!

Pour us your poison, let us be comforted!
Once we have burned our brains out, we can plunge
to Hell or Heaven—any abyss will do—
deep in the Unknown to find the *new*!

ADDITIONAL POEMS

1 ✹ THE FOUNTAIN

Your eyes are tired, poor lover—close them, then;
lie still, just as you are, in that casual pose
where pleasure found you, took you, let you go!
Down in the courtyard the fountain whispers on,
never falling silent, day or night—
an echo of the ecstasy that was
this evening's overwhelming gift of love.

    The wisp of water rises,
        wavers, reappears:
           a white bouquet
           whose flowers sway
    until the moon releases
        showers of bright tears.

So it is with your soul that, set aglow
and glorified by the flash of pleasure shared,
surges swift and valiant to the skies
that hale it to their vast enchanted height,
then sinks back, dying in a slow descent
of languor that by melancholy ways
ebbs to the inmost center of my heart.

    The wisp of water rises,
        wavers, reappears:
           a white bouquet
           where flowers sway
    until the moon releases
        showers of bright tears.

Lover, whom the darkness so becomes
that I rejoice to lie upon your breast
and listen to the never-ending plaint
that murmurs to itself in marble pools
among the trees disheveled by the wind:

moon, melodious water, marvelous night—
your sorrow is the mirror of my love!

The wisp of water rises,
wavers, reappears:
a white bouquet
whose flowers sway
until the moon releases
showers of bright tears.

2 ❋ **Berthe: Her Eyes**

No other eyes can bear comparison!
Something of Night is in your glance, my child;
a gentle darkness falls and fills and flees—
O world of charming shadows, fall on me!

Great eyes of my child, beloved shrines,
you make me think of those enchanted caves
where out of the lethargic mysteries
neglected treasures tenuously shine.

The eyes of my child are secret and immense
as you are, boundless Night—lit up like you
with stars that are the dreams of Love and Faith,
whose depths are luminous, alluring, chaste...

3 ❋ **Hymn**

To Love in all her loveliness
filling my heart with light,
to the Angel, the Idol, the Muse,
homage and endless praise!

Who like a salt-wind from the sea
suffuses life with joy

and pours into my unslaked heart
    eternity's bouquet!

What is your substance, flawless Love?
    Who can pronounce your name,
invisible grain of musk at the core
    of my immortal soul?

Sachet forever fresh that scents
    this intimate retreat,
forgotten censer smoking still
    in secret through the dark!

To Love who by her favor grants
    my health and happiness,
to the Angel, the Idol, the Muse,
    homage and endless praise!

4 ❋   THE PROMISES OF A FACE

I love, pale Beauty, how the shadows mass
    beneath the arches of your brow;
black as they are, those eyes of yours inspire
    anything but funereal thoughts—

eyes that languishingly show the way
    out of that labyrinth of hair,
eyes that intimate: "If you desire,
    lover of the modeled muse,

to realize the hopes that we arouse
    and sate the tastes that you profess,
rely on what you see: descend, explore
    a matching nether opulence;

you'll find at the tip of each imposing breast
    a medal cast in massy bronze,

and where the belly's sulfur silk is seamed
    with saffron velvet, flourishes

a sinuous fleece that is in fact the twin
    of that enormous head of hair—
and which in darkness rivals you, O Night,
    deep and spreading starless Night!"

5 ❀   **THREE EPIGRAPHS**

ON A PORTRAIT OF HONORÉ DAUMIER

The man whose image is presented here
and who by the most penetrating art
affords us means of laughing at ourselves—
this man, dear reader, is a philosopher.

He mocks us—true, he is a satirist,
and yet the energy with which he paints
(or etches) Evil and its aftermath
demonstrates the beauty of his heart.

His mirth is the reverse of Melmoth's sneer
or the snickering of Mephistopheles,
licked by the lurid light of a Fury's torch
that burns them to a crisp but leaves us cold—

a glance at their glee shows it for what it is,
a painful caricature of gaiety;
while Daumier's spreads like sunlight, glad and free,
a sign of kindness, evidence of grace.

ON MANET'S PORTRAIT 'LOLA DE VALENCE'

Among so many Beauties, you might think
Desire confused, yet it abandons them

all for Lola flashing black and pink
iridescence of a secret gem...

ON DELACROIX'S 'TASSO IN PRISON'

The poet in the dungeon—ragged, sick,
and trampling on a manuscript in shreds—
measures with a panic-stricken glare
the dizzying stairs that swallow up his soul.

Beguiled by ghostly laughter in the air
his reason falters, grasps at phantom straws;
Doubt besieges him and imbecile Fears
in hideous yet ever-changing shapes...

This genius confined in a filthy hole,
these shrieks and grimaces, the spectral swarm
gibbering spitefully behind his ear,

this dreamer whom the madhouse horror wakes—
here is your emblem, visionary soul,
smothered by Reality between four walls!

6 ❋ THE VOICE

Above my cradle loomed the bookcase where
Latin ashes and the dust of Greece
mingled with novels, history, and verse
in one dark Babel. I was folio-high
when I first heard the voices. "All the world,"
said one, insidious but sure, "is cake—
let me make you an appetite to match,
and then your happiness need have no end."
And the other: "Come, O come with me in dreams
beyond the possible, beyond the known!"
that second voice sang like the wind in the reeds,
a wandering phantom out of nowhere, sweet

to hear yet somehow horrifying too.
"Now and forever!" I answered, whereupon
my wound was with me—ever since, my Fate:
behind the scenes, the frivolous decors
of all existence, deep in the abyss,
I see distinctly other, brighter worlds;
yet victimized by what I know I see,
I sense the serpent coiling at my heels;
and therefore, like the prophets, from that hour
I've loved the wilderness, I've loved the sea;
no ordinary sadness touches me
though I find savor in the bitterest wine;
how many truths I trade away for lies,
and musing on heaven stumble over trash…
Even so, the voice consoles me: "Keep your dreams,
the wise have none so lovely as the mad."

7 ❋   THE UNFORESEEN

A miser watches while his father dies
and speculates, before the corpse is cold:
"There must be some old boards out in the shed—
    good enough for such a thing!"

A coquette coos to herself: "My heart is kind,
and naturally God gave me looks to match."
Her heart! that organ shriveled like a ham
    cured in Hell's eternal fire!

A fuming scribbler—ask *him*: he's a torch!—
taunts his readers drowned in a sea of ink:
"Where has He gone, this loving God of yours,
    where is the Savior you profess?"

Better still, I know one libertine
who wrings his hands and snivels night and day,

repeating helplessly: "I will be good—
    starting first thing tomorrow!"

The clock in the tower whispers: "It is time.
Useless to warn them—flesh is deaf and blind,
and fragile as a termite-ridden wall
    the grubs have eaten from within."

Whereupon appears One they had all denied—
their gloating accuser: "I trust that you enjoyed
taking communion from my chamber-pot
    at our charming little Black Mass?

Each of you in his heart has worshipped me,
in secret kissed my filthy ass—behold!
Hear my laugh and welcome Satan home,
    huge and ugly as the earth itself!

Red-handed hypocrites, how could you hope
to diddle your Master out of his reward?
As if *two* prizes were given: being rich
    and reaching Heaven besides!

His prey must make it worth the hunter's while
to stalk such game so long out in the cold.
Now you will learn just how much misery
    loves company—come down!

down with me through layers of mud and dust,
down through the rubble of your rotting graves
into my palace carved from a single rock
    without one soft spot in its heart,

made as it is of universal Sin:
it holds my pain, my glory and my pride!"
—Meanwhile perched above the universe
    an Angel trumpets the victory

of those whose hearts exclaim: "O Lord, my God!
I bless Thy rod, I thank Thee for this pain!
My soul in Thy hands is more than a futile toy,
    and Thy wisdom is infinite."

That trumpet's sound is so magnificent
on solemn eves of Heavenly harvesting,
that like an ecstasy it gladdens those
    whose praises it proclaims.

8 ✳ TO A MALABAR GIRL

Your feet are agile as your hands; your hips
make well-endowed white women envious;
your velvet eyes are blacker than your flesh,
and for the artist pondering his theme
your body is a blessing undisguised.
Livening hot blue landscapes where you live,
you fill the water jugs and perfume jars,
you light your master's pipe and wave away
mosquitoes from his bed—such are your tasks,
and when the plane-trees rustle in the dawn
you buy bananas ripe from the bazaar.
The day is filled with the sound of your bare feet
and snatches of incomprehensible songs;
when evening's scarlet mantle falls, you stretch
your limbs out on the matting, and you dream—
what do you dream? There must be hummingbirds
and bright hibiscus lovely as yourself...

Poor happy child! You want to visit France,
that crowded country where no one is well?
Make your farewells to swaying tamarinds
and trust your life to sailors and the sea?
Dressed in nothing but those muslin rags
you'd shiver out your days beneath the snow—
how you would weep for carefree nakedness,

your supple body cruelly corseted
as you hustled supper in the city's mud,
selling the fragrance of your foreign charms,
sad-eyed and yearning through our filthy fogs
for the scattered ghosts of absent coconut palms!

9 ✴   A LONG WAY FROM HERE

This is the place—the holy hut
where, always in her Sunday best
and elbow-deep in cushions, she

waits for us—or anyone—to call,
listening to the fountains sob
and fanning her unbridled breast;

we are in Dorothea's room—
nearby, the wind and water sing
a tearful sort of cradle-song
to pacify this pampered child.

Dedicated downward strokes
massage her skin to burnished teak
with oil of musk and benjamin
—and all our tribute flowers swoon.

10 ✴   ROMANTIC SUNSET

The sun is all very well when it rises—then
who minds returning its abrupt salute?
But fortunate the man who still can find
room in his heart for its high-flown farewell!

Take my case. I have seen all nature swoon
under that gaze, like an over-driven heart.

Late as it is, who can resist the West
and the hope of entertaining one last ray...

No use following! The god withdraws,
and darkness comes into its own. The world
is cold and wet and full of mysteries;

a mortuary odor fouls the marsh
where my uncertain footsteps try to keep
from squashing frogs or snakes or something worse...

11 ❀   SCRUTINY AT MIDNIGHT

The clock ironically summons us
to account for what we did with this day past,
Friday the thirteenth, ominous date! and yet,
knowing the risks, we have defiled our life—

blasphemed the most incontestable of Gods
and (worthy slave of Hell) like a parasite
at Croesus's feast, to please our monstrous host,
mocked what we love and what we loathe acclaimed!

oppressed the weak we wrongfully despise
and (servile bully) cringed to stupid Power,
genuflected before the throne of Things
and blessed the phosphorescence of decay!

Last, to cheat our moods with madness, we
whose Muse's priesthood serves a world of death
have drunk without thirst and eaten without hunger!
—Let darkness hide us: quick, blow out the lamp!

12 ✿ SAD MADRIGAL

I

What does it matter to me that you are wise?
    Be lovely—and be sad!
Tears are an advantage to the face,
as streams enhance the meadow's mystery
    and rains refresh the rose.

I love you best of all when happiness
    fades from your downcast brow;
when horror overflows your heart; and when
your days are darkened by a spreading cloud:
    the shadow of the past.

I love you when your brimming eyes release
    teardrops hot as blood;
when all my consolations fail, and pain
is more than your tormented life can bear:
    a deathbed agony.

I drink up every tear you weep—they are
    the holiest joy I know,
the truest hymn, the most delicious draught:
deep in your heart I see them shining still,
    the pearls shed by your eyes!

2

I know your heart, that crowded solitude
    where old uprooted loves
are crammed into a roaring forge: you nurse
beneath your breast a semblance of the pride
    that purifies the damned;

yet not until your dreams, my dear, reflect
    the fires of Hell itself,
the nightmares you can never waken from
for all your faith in poison and the noose,
    in powder, shot, and steel;

not until you cower at each knock
    and dread the air you breathe,
shuddering each time you hear the clock,
will you have known the merciless embrace
    of absolute Disgust—

then, only then, my slave, my queen,
    whose love for me is fear,
your soul half-stifled by the tainted night,
will you turn to me and sob the words: "I am
    your equal, O my King!"

13 ❋   THE REBEL

An angry Angel plunges out of the sky,
grips the sinner's hair and shakes him hard,
shouting: "Hear and obey, it is the law!
I am your Guardian Angel. Do my will!

Learn that you must love, with all your heart,
the poor in body and spirit, the low, the lost,
so that your charity may spread for Christ
a proper carpet when He walks the earth.

Such is true love! Before your heart goes numb,
let the glory of God awaken it to joy,
for that alone among your pleasures lasts!"

And the Angel, punishing to prove his love,
torments his victim with his giant fists;
but still the damned soul answers: "I will not!"

14 ❋ A PAGAN'S PRAYER

No, no less than the worst of your fires will do
to warm my sluggish heart to life again...
Pleasure! sensual Pleasure, scourge of souls:
Diva, supplicem exaudi! Grant me pain!

Goddess brightening the air we breathe,
flame in the darkness following our feet,
hear the petition of a fallen soul
who consecrates to you a brazen song.

Pleasure, sensual Pleasure! Be my queen
forever! Wear the siren mask of flesh
and velvet that beguiles the skull beneath,

or fill my goblet with your heavy sleep
that shimmers in the mysteries of wine,
Pleasure, shifting phantom, shameless Muse!

15 ❋ MEDITATION

Behave, my Sorrow! let's have no more scenes.
Evening's what you wanted—Evening's here:
a gradual darkness overtakes the town,
bringing peace to some, to others pain.

Now, while humanity racks up remorse
in low distractions under Pleasure's lash,
groveling for a ruthless master—come
away, my Sorrow, leave them! Give me your hand...

See how the dear departed dowdy years
crowd the balconies of heaven, leaning down,
while smiling out of the sea appears Regret;

the Sun will die in its sleep beneath a bridge,
and trailing westward like a winding-sheet—
listen, my dear—how softly Night arrives.

16 ❁ THE ABYSS

Pascal had his abyss, it followed him.
But the abyss is All—action and dream,
language, desire!—and who could count the times
the wind of Fear has made my blood run cold!

Each way I turn, above me and below,
tempting and terrible too the silence, the space...
By night God traces with a knowing hand
unending nightmares on unending dark.

I balk at sleep as if it were a hole
filled up with horrors, leading God knows where;
my windows open on Infinity,

and haunted by its vertigo my mind
envies the indifference of the void:
will Numbers and Beings never set me free!

17 ❁ ICARUS LAMENTS

Happy men who fornicate with whores
          are satisfied and fit,
while my exhausted arms are impotent
          from clasping only clouds;

nights of staring at the peerless stars
          that ornament the dark
have seared my eyes until they see no more
          than memories of suns;

I have not hollowed out the heart of space
          nor touched its boundaries:
beneath a fiery gaze I cannot meet
          I feel my pinions fail;

I burn for beauty, but I shall not have
          the highest accolade—
my name will not be given to the abyss
          that waits to be my grave.

18 * THE LID

Wherever he goes—on land or out to sea,
under a flaming sun or a frozen sky—
servant of Jesus, Aphrodite's slave,
Midas in splendor, mendicant in rags,

city-mouse, country-mouse, anchored or adrift,
whether his wits are vacuous or keen,
man lives in terror of the Mystery
and casts a trembling glance above his head

to heaven—Heavens! the vault that walls him in,
illuminated ceiling of a music hall
where every walk-on treads a bloody board;

the hermit's hope, the libertine's despair—
the Sky! black lid of that enormous pot
in which innumerable generations boil.

19 * THE OFFENDED MOON

Worshipped once, discreetly, by our sires
as Cynthia, the lamp of secret haunts,
and still attended through blue landscapes
by a blameless harem of the stars, O moon!

do you see the lovers on their prosperous beds,
teeth gleaming where they sleep open-mouthed?
Do you see the poet struggling with his lines?
Or the vipers coupling in the new-mown hay?

Creeping on high in your yellow domino,
do you still, from darkness until dawn,
search out Endymion's outdated charms?

—"What I see is your mother, child of this ruined age,
bent to her looking-glass by the weight of years
and skillfully painting the breast that suckled you!"

20 ✳ EPIGRAPH FOR A BANNED BOOK

Gentle reader, being—as you are—
a cautious man of uncorrupted tastes,
lay aside this disobliging work,
as orgiastic as it is abject.

Unless you've graduated from the school
of Satan (devil of a pedagogue!)
the poems will be Greek to you, or else
you'll set me down for one more raving fool.

If, however, your impassive eye
can plunge into the chasms on each page,
read on, my friend: you'll learn to love me yet.

Inquiring spirit, fellow-sufferer
in search, even here, of your own Paradise,
pity me...If not, to Hell with you!

CHARLES BAUDELAIRE (1821–1867) was a French poet who also produced notable work as an essayist, art critic, and pioneering translator of Edgar Allan Poe. *Les Fleurs du Mal* (*The Flowers of Evil*), his most famous work, expresses the changing nature of beauty in the rapidly industrializing Paris during the mid-nineteenth century. Baudelaire's highly original style of prose-poetry influenced a whole generation of poets including Paul Verlaine, Arthur Rimbaud, and many others. He is credited with coining the term "modernity" (*modernité*) to designate the fleeting, ephemeral experience of life in an urban metropolis, and the responsibility of artistic expression to capture that experience.

RICHARD HOWARD is a distinguished poet, critic, and translator who holds a unique place in contemporary American letters: he is credited with introducing modern French fiction—particularly examples of the Nouveau Roman—to the American public. Howard won the Pulitzer Prize in Poetry in 1970. His other honors include the American Book Award, the Harriet Monroe Memorial Prize, the PEN Translation Medal, the Levinson Prize, the title of Chevalier from France's L'Ordre National du Merite, and the position of Poet Laureate of New York from 1993 to 1995. He served as the poetry editor of *The Paris Review* and *Western Humanities Review* for many years.